Successfully Sell Your Business:

Expert Advice from a Business Broker

By Andrew Rogerson

Certified Business Intermediary (CBI)
Certified Business Broker (CBB)
Certified Machinery and Equipment Appraiser (CMEA)
Certified Senior Business Analyst (CSBA)

www.Andrew-Rogerson.com

Published by
RBS
Rogerson Business Services
Sacramento, CA
www.businesstransactionbooks.com

Rogerson Business Services
777 Campus Commons Road, Suite 200
Sacramento, CA, 95825
www.businesstransactionbooks.com

Successfully Buy Your Business: Expert Advice from a Business Broker

ISBN: 978-1441478146

Library of Congress Registration Number: TX-7-071-315

Disclaimer

This publication is designed to provide accurate and helpful information on selling a business. It is sold with the understanding that the author is NOT engaged in offering legal, accounting or any other professional advice. Please consult a competent professional for assistance.

Acknowledgements

The Resource Handbook for Business Brokers and Intermediaries by Tom West
The Business Reference Guide by Tom West
Business Brokerage Press
Len Krick, United Business Brokers, Las Vegas, NV
Ultimate Guide to Personal Finance for Entrepreneurs by Peter Sander with J Jeff Lambert
Exit: A business Owner's Guide to Selling a Company by Alexander Vantarakis & William Whitehurst
Business Brokerage by Lloyd R Manning
Roger Murphy at Murphy Business and Financial Corporation, Clearwater, FL
International Business Brokers Association (IBBA)
California Association of Business Brokers (CABB)
Monty Watson, Walker Advisory Associates

Special Thanks

Special thanks to the following for contributing to the text and/or checking the details: Anne Rogerson, John Rogerson, Tony Gilbert, Roger Murphy, Tim Rogers, Jerry Tsai and Fred Hall. Also, a special thanks to Stephanie Chandler for the professional editing of this guide. Stephanie offered many thoughts and suggestions to improve and enhance the guide.

Stephanie Chandler
Pro Publishing Services
11230 Gold River Drive, #310-413
Gold River, CA, 95670
http://www.ProPublishingServices.com

Also, an extra special thanks to Anne Rogerson and Belinda Rogerson for their editing and work on the website.

Special Acknowledgment of IBBA

The International Business Brokers Association is a global organization that advances the professional development of over 1,800 member intermediaries, educates potential clients about the value of intermediary services, and promotes the highest possible standards of ethical conduct. IBBA sponsors national education programs and conferences twice each year and cooperates with state and local business broker's organizations to conduct "grass roots" programs for the benefit of business communities around the country. IBBA awards the prestigious designation of Certified Business Intermediary (CBI) to members who demonstrate professional excellence through their intermediary experience and education and pass a comprehensive examination. Andrew Rogerson holds the CBI designation.

For more information contact:

International Business Brokers Association
401 North Michigan Avenue, 24th Floor
Chicago, IL 60611-4267
Phone: 888-686-4222   Fax: 312-673-6599
E-mail: admin@ibba.org
Web: www.ibba.org

Special Acknowledgment of CABB

The California Association of Business Brokers is a professional trade association whose members are actively involved in assisting their clients in buying, selling, and evaluating businesses. CABB was organized to recognize the professionals of business opportunity brokerage, to help educate the public on the benefits of using licensed intermediaries, and to establish a code of ethics to which members adhere. CABB awards the prestigious designation of Certified Business Broker (CBB) to members who demonstrate professional excellence through their intermediary and business brokerage experience and education and pass a series of examinations. Andrew Rogerson holds the CBB designation.

For more information contact:

California Association of Business Brokers
1215 K Street, Suite 2290
Sacramento, CA, 95814
Phone: 866-972-2220 Fax: 916-231-2141
E-mail: cabb@cabb.org
Web: www.cabb.org

Table Of Contents

Welcome!

Trying to sell a business is arguably one of the most difficult sales a business owner will encounter. This guide has two main purposes. The first is to provide information about the different tasks and questions business owners may come across when selling a business. The second purpose is to provide a means for a seller to plan, get organized and be ready when selling their business in order to be better prepared and understand what's happening at each point in the transaction.

The inspiration for this guide comes from my personal experiences in buying, selling, owning and operating five businesses in two countries, researching many, many different types of businesses, and my current experience as a business consultant and business broker to those that wish to exit or enter business ownership. Additionally, the guide uses the techniques advocated by the International Business Brokers Association (IBBA). I wish someone had given me some organized structure to tackle this difficult experience as I have had to learn it all the hard way. Now my goal is to help make that journey easier for you.

There are so many nuances to selling a business. Each transaction is unique in that it brings together not only the different experiences of the buyers and sellers and their families, but also the attorneys, accountants, landlords, finance companies, appraisers, intermediaries/brokers and other professionals that may assist in the transaction.

Please use this workbook to make notes along the way. This is a guide to read, learn and stimulate so you can write down thoughts and check them out later so that you can be better prepared. If you prefer to scribble notes before finalizing your thoughts, photocopy the pages so you can have one final version to work through as you arrive at different decision points in the transaction.

Just so I am clear, if you fill in the pages in the guide and then have one buyer that comes along and buys the business in the exact order I have written, you are a very lucky person. You should expect to talk with different people with different life and business experiences. If you expect the transaction to flow EXACTLY as it is outlined in this guide, then you will be disappointed. However, if you follow the steps as closely as possible you will have a much greater chance of success. So be patient as you travel your journey of selling your business.

The Golden Rule

When selling your business, put yourself in the shoes of the buyer and see things from their perspective.

Let's Get Started: Your Goals

Use the chart below to write down major tasks that come to mind that you feel you must do to successfully sell your business. Refer back to this chart as you read through this guide so that you can add tasks you want to complete and stay up-to-date.

Task Description	Start Date	Completion Date

Idea Tracker

As you read this guide, it will inspire ideas or prompt action items. Use the space below to jot down and track these ideas so you can organize your thoughts into action items.

Your Feedback

The goal of this guide is to help small business owners through the process of selling their business in the quickest time possible for the best price possible. Although all business sellers have the same objective—to sell their business—the journey to achieving that goal is never the same.

There are a wide variety of factors that affect the entire process:

    ✓ Sellers and buyers have unique personal differences.
    ✓ The professional support services each party hires may come into conflict.
    ✓ The direction of the economy has impact beyond anyone's control.
    ✓ The current state of the industry the business is a part of can have a positive or a negative impact.
    ✓ Taxes and related laws often change.

Because of these factors and many others, I strongly advise you to seek the assistance of experts when it comes time to actually sell or purchase a business.

If you have comments or suggestions that you feel would improve this guide and you have a moment to share, please e-mail your suggestions to info@andrew-rogerson.com.

With thanks,

Andrew Rogerson

Section One

General Information

"*Be curious always! For knowledge will not acquire you: you must acquire it.*"

Dr. John G. Hibben

Introduction

The steps to selling a business are numerous, often complex and at times, very frustrating. The major purpose of this guide is to outline and explain the many steps, why they need to be taken, and when to take them. With this information, this guide can reduce the number of steps or missteps that you may take during the process of selling your business, thereby reducing the costs, complexity and frustration.

And remember this guide is built for work. Make notes and use the templates to jot down ideas as they come to mind so you can refer back to them. The selling of your business is unique. One of the main reasons for publishing this in workbook format is so that you can write in it, customize and use the information to be successful in selling your business in the quickest time possible, for the highest price and at the lowest cost.

The flow of the guide is as follows:
- ✓ Section one provides some general information on some of the concepts and terms you may come across when selling your business.
- ✓ Section two introduces tax, legal, accounting and business valuation topics and how they relate to selling a business.
- ✓ Section three allows you to specifically look at your business and do some research on each topic as well as apply ideas from sections one and two.
- ✓ Sections four through eight provide an overview of the process that I would follow as a business broker when listing and selling a business.
- ✓ Section nine provides a financial recasting exercise for the curious.
- ✓ Section ten provides additional information on financing and a sample Ethics Agreement and Confidentiality Agreement.
- ✓ The last section includes a glossary of terms so that you can better understand the industry terminology.

Please write down any terms you come across that aren't familiar to you. If they aren't covered in the glossary, you are welcome to e-mail them to me at info@andrew-rogerson.com and I will add them to the next edition of the guide. You are also welcome to e-mail questions about selling your business.

Business Advisors

There are different professionals that may participate in the process of buying and selling a business. Attorneys, accountants, financial planners, appraisers, commercial real estate agents, business brokers and merger and acquisition (M&A) consultants are just some of the many professionals that you may consult.

Each market segment tends to have its own business jargon and methodologies. For example, a business broker tends to work in Discretionary Earnings or Sellers Discretionary Earnings or Discretionary Cash Flow whereas an M&A consultant tends to work in EBIDTA or EBIT multiples. Have I lost you already or am I making little sense? If these terms seem confusing, you are not alone. But don't let the jargon used exclude you from understanding what is happening in the sale of your business. Just as it is difficult to understand when someone speaks a foreign language, professionals can use industry jargon or buzzwords to exclude you or try to inflate their importance. This is your business and your life so if this happens, stop the conversation and ask for an explanation. As I mentioned earlier, don't forget the glossary of terms at the back of this guide as it may assist you.

Jargon And Buzzwords

Write down industry jargon or buzzwords you want to research and better understand.

Publicly Traded Company vs. Privately Held Company

This guide is written for the owner of a privately held company and has no relevance for selling publicly traded companies or stocks.

Privately Held Companies and Gross Sales

Within the domain of privately held companies there are different sub groups. A privately held company with annual sales of $30 million or more will be valued differently than a company with annual gross sales between $2 million and $10 million. Annual gross sales between $750,000 and $2 million or annual gross sales less than $750,000 also have different values and chances for selling.

This can be readily seen from the table below. But if you look closer at the table, and in particular at the last two columns, there is some interesting information. The businesses with annual sales less than $750,000 have approximately 884,000 businesses for sale at any one time. Of those businesses, only 157,000 of those businesses will sell—or 1 in 5.5. Similarly, businesses with annual sales between $750,000 and $2 million have approximately 173,000 businesses for sale at any one time with 1 in 4 or 25% of those businesses actually selling.

U.S. Businesses for Sale and How Many Actually Sell

Annual Revenue (000)	Number of Employees	Priced (000)	Percent of all Businesses	Number of Businesses (000)	Number for Sale	Number that Sell
<$750	<10	<$500	80%	4,376	884,000 1 in 5	157,000 1 in 5.5
$750 to $2,000	10—20	$500 to $3,000	9%	590	173,000 1 in 3.5	43,000 1 in 4
$2,000 to $30,000	21—100	$3,000 to $20,000	8%	490	73,000 1 in 7	21,000 1 in 3.5
> $30,000	> 100	> $20,000	3%	50	9,000 1 in 6	2,500 1 in 3

Source: Business Brokerage Press

Ethics And Confidentiality

If this is the first time you are selling a business and therefore dealing with buyers and the professionals that work in the different industries, you will have no choice but to consider the question of ethics. It is not an issue that is always addressed, but as you are dealing with personal property and an entity that can easily be damaged, ethics are a consideration. My suggestion is to use an Ethics Agreement so it is clear the position you are taking, what you are offering and what you expect in return.

A sample Ethics Agreement is included in section ten.

Confidentiality

Most business brokers will insist that potential buyers of your business sign a Confidentiality Agreement (or Non Disclosure Agreement) before discussing any information about your business.

In some situations, in addition to a Confidentiality Agreement, the potential buyer may be asked to provide a financial statement to demonstrate their ability to get a loan to buy the business. The financial statement will discourage some buyers from taking their inquiry any further. A genuine buyer should understand the sensitivity of the material they are asking to see and understand that the business owner only wants that information revealed to qualified parties.

Confidentiality is crucial because a business is a very fragile entity. It generally involves family members, customers, suppliers, employees, banks or credit providers, landlords, franchisors and other parties. Here are some potential concerns:

- ✓ If a supplier finds out a business is for sale, they may withdraw a line of credit.
- ✓ Employees get concerned about a new owner as they may no longer have a job.
- ✓ Landlords get concerned that the new owner may not be able to pay the rent on time.
- ✓ Customers get concerned because they know the current owner but don't know if they can expect the same service from a new owner.
- ✓ Competitors love to know a business is being sold so they can use it to their advantage. For example, they may suggest to customers that the current owner is selling because they are not making any money or they don't know what they are doing.

And the list goes on. I would always recommend using a Confidentiality Agreement to protect your business because it aids in sorting out the serious buyers from those that just want to look and gossip. A sample Confidentiality Agreement is included in section ten.

Reasons For Selling

Timing

According to the International Business Brokers Association, now that the Baby Boomer generation is starting to retire, the expectation is that a lot of businesses will change hands as business owners seek to cash out retirement funds from their businesses.

A lot of business owners have spent their entire lives caring for, nurturing and protecting their "baby" so selling can be one of the most difficult and emotional decisions they make. Selling the business is also an admission the owner is getting older and heading to retirement. Therefore, the ultimate timing and reason for selling must feel right to the seller so that they can emotionally let go and hand over the business to a new owner.

Other Reasons for Selling

Retirement won't be the only reason for selling. Other reasons include:
1. Health issues
2. Divorce or legal issue forcing a sale
3. Partners no longer able to work with each other
4. Owner burnout
5. Alignment of the "economic stars"—the owner believes they have the business achieving its highest potential with their skill set and so it is time to sell and take on a new challenge
6. Lack of operating capital and need for more capital to grow
7. Key employee loss prevention strategy
8. Declining sales and/or cash flow

Expectations: Seller Vs Buyer

Following is an example to help put the expectations of the seller and the buyer in perspective.

The seller expects to:
1. Receive all cash up front;
2. Provide one week of training;
3. Provide the buyer with one day to do their due diligence;
4. Close the offer the day after the completion of due diligence;
5. Be paid five to six times the business earnings or discretionary earnings.

The buyer expects to:
1. Buy a business with 10% down payment;
2. Receive two months of training free of charge from the seller;
3. Have four weeks to complete their due diligence;
4. Work in the business for 30 days to "test drive" it;
5. Pay no more than one year's worth of business earnings or discretionary earnings.

About where the seller and the buyer meet:
1. The down payment from the buyer is about equal to the business earnings or discretionary earnings;
2. Seller provides some financing;
3. Seller provides two to three weeks of training;
4. Buyer receives two weeks to complete their due diligence;
5. It takes 45 to 60 days to close;
6. The business is sold between two to three times earnings.

Disclose, Disclose, Disclose

You've heard or read the maxim that real estate is about location, location, location. When selling a business that maxim is *disclose, disclose, disclose* — once you have received a signed Confidentiality Agreement from your buyer.

I would suggest that more transactions die because one party doesn't feel the other party is telling the truth or hiding information. It is my experience that business owners are more apt to tell the truth because that's what business in general demands. Additionally, because of this, business owners are quicker at developing a sense about whether someone is being honest with them or not. As a result, honest people like to deal with honest people. And one final thought: disclose as much as possible early in the transaction. If a buyer senses that information has been withheld, that can often be a deal-breaker.

Types Of Buyer

Each buyer who inquires about your business will probably have their own unique reason for wanting to buy. By talking with the buyer, understanding their needs and then placing them in one of the categories below, you can understand what they are looking for so you are better prepared to discuss and negotiate the transaction.

Individual Buyer

This is generally one person with good financial resources and background or experience for managing and leading a particular business in a particular industry. This type of buyer is usually looking for a particular business that is financially healthy. They are looking for a return on their investment and some flexibility in lifestyle choices. They also believe they can buy and at least maintain the current performance of the business or take it to a higher level.

Corporate Executive

This is a buyer who has many years of service with a large corporation and has concerns that downsizing may occur. In some cases, they are getting older and have their retirement money tucked away and would like to see what it would be like to run their own business. Franchise businesses are particularly attractive to them as they like the structure and organization that comes from working in this business model.

Existing Employee

The buyer of a business can be an existing employee. If the business has a strong cash flow and the employee is able to put together a small down payment with the seller carrying back some of the financing, this can be a mutually beneficial arrangement. SBA financing may be an option here—especially if the employee has management expertise.

Investment Buyer or Financial Buyer

All buyers want a return on their investment. However, with investment or financial buyers this is their primary motivation. Their ability to get financing on as large part of the purchase price as possible is also motivating. They have less interest in the type of industry and many of the specifics of the business operation.

Synergistic Buyer

This is usually a company and their purpose of buying the business is their belief that joining the two companies will produce more, or be worth more, together than if the two companies were to remain separate.

Industry Buyer

This type of buyer is often a competitor or owns a very similar operation. They know the industry well and therefore see little value in paying for the expertise and skill of the seller.

Strategic Buyer

Like the synergistic buyer, the strategic buyer is usually a business owner with a goal to expand their current company. They leverage their expertise to enter into new markets by acquiring market share and then increase market share through the acquisition. Their strategy can also include deploying a new technology and/or eliminating a competitor or some competitive element.

Types Of Buyer Personalities

Just as there are different types of buyers with different motivations, there are also buyers with different types of personalities. Understanding these different personality types may help you decide how best to work with them. These assessments come from my own experience and provide a little "tongue in cheek" perspective.

Unemployed

This is the best type of buyer provided they have the money or enough down payment and a good credit score. They are motivated and generally want to move quickly to make a decision and start earning an income again.

Engineer

This will be the hardest buyer that you work with. They invariably have the money and the skills to run a business, but they have a need to know absolutely every piece of information about the economy, industry and your business. Many meetings are required and each is long and laborious. Questions that are answered in the first three meetings are asked in subsequent meetings and if the answers are slightly different from what was said earlier, the buyer wants to know why and then go back and revisit every other question around that topic. Their chances of taking the emotional risk to buy a business are very low as after all the questions are answered, they find it impossible to commit by signing their name to the check to buy the business.

Talker

This person loves to talk. They have great personality and charm and you think they are the perfect person for the business. They are pleasant to deal with, ask polite and relevant questions, are genuinely interested in being liked and making sure they fit in. There is only one problem—they don't have any money and can therefore be a huge time waster. Watch talkers carefully as they are such good talkers you are afraid to say no or offended them.

Know-It-All

Another problem buyer is the know-it-all. They are like talkers but not as diplomatic. They have a bunch of knowledge making them sound like a great candidate as they "get it" and the industry and your business. They probably have money, it is just that they are hard to get along with as they love to tell you what they are going to do to make the business better and at the same time they have no problem in suggesting changes you should make now or telling you what you are not doing right.

Job Seeker

Try to establish this one early on as they are a complete time waster. Asking for a financial statement generally takes care of them. They have no money and no ambition. They don't like their current job so if they find the perfect business with zero down payment they will be made. There's quite a few job seekers out there so flush these out early.

Investor Using Other People's Money

This one is worse than the talker or the know-it-all. The investor using other people's money presents himself as a cash buyer or leader of an investment syndicate authorized to check out viable businesses for sale. Once again they can be a time waster so isolate them quickly. The best way to do that is by either requesting a financial statement or request a meeting of all parties that are investing in the business. If the investor lives interstate or overseas you have your answer—would you lend money to a friend or family member to buy a business you will rarely see?

Savior

This one's a bit like the talker or the know-it-all as he/she is going to buy the business to turn it around and keep the jobs of all the employees. The quickest way to isolate this one is to ask for a financial statement as they won't have any money.

All Cash

The all cash buyer is tricky because you so want to believe they are genuine and that your business is the perfect match for them. They know this, hence the reason they claim to be a cash buyer. However, all they do is waste your time because the cash doesn't exist. If they had that much cash, they would use that money to buy a more expensive business that produces a greater cash flow.

One of the all cash buyer's tricky behaviors is to convince you that they are genuine and then use the lure of being a cash buyer to reduce your price. It is very easy to flush this buyer out—simply ask for a verification of funds and make sure the proof is an original document—not a photocopy. It is perfectly fine that they redact the account number or other sensitive information.

Obstinate

This one is really easy to identify: lots of talk, lots of promises and seemingly the perfect buyer (similar to the all cash buyer). But the obstinate buyer refuses to sign the confidentiality agreement. The solution to this one is really simple. Move on and don't waste any more time with them. If someone refuses to sign a confidentiality agreement, imagine how difficult they will be when you are getting into detailed negotiations.

---

8 Reasons Why a Business Does Not Sell

1. The seller starts off thinking he is serious about selling but gets into the process and sees how difficult it can be and then changes his mind.
2. The seller fears having nothing to do after the sale and changes his mind. Going to work and running the business provides structure and familiarity. Once the business sells, that will go away and so fear stops the seller from moving forward.
3. Receiving few or no offers after listing the business for sale. The seller thinks he may not get what the business is worth and removes it from sale.
4. The next phase of life the seller had planned, such as going back to school or looking after the grandkids, suddenly seems less appealing than continuing with the business.
5. The seller thought he had the best business in the world and would receive all cash. When that doesn't happen, he decides not to sell.
6. Due diligence disclosed an environmental, government or legal issue outside the risk tolerance of the buyer.
7. The seller wants too much for the business and isn't willing to accept what the market is willing to pay.
8. The seller cannot provide the necessary books and records to support income, expenses and profit.

Franchises

According to the International Franchise Association, franchises account for 40% of all retail sales in the US, franchise businesses were responsible for over $1.5 trillion in economic output and a new franchise opens every 8 minutes of every business day. The point here is that franchising is a major force into today's economy. If you own a franchise and are considering selling it, just as with a privately held business, there will be many steps to take and prepare your franchise for sale.

For clarity, in using the term franchise, I am not just referring to a business operating under a Uniform Franchise Offering Circular (UFOC) and soon to be called a Franchise Disclosure Document. This term includes corporations that license their brand or companies that own a trademark or patent and allow this to be used. For example, some oil companies license their brand. Companies that license their brand may have specific requirements so make sure you explore and fully understand the offer. Otherwise you may waste a lot of time and create a lot of frustration trying to close a deal with a buyer that will never be approved.

Tip: Prepare for Questions

Never leave a question unanswered –
the buyer will think you are trying to hide something.

End Of Chapter Notes

Use this page to write down notes, ideas and other brainstorming for selling your business.

Section Two

Education

"*Education is the ability to meet life's situations.*"

Dr. John G. Hibben

Introduction

The purpose of section two is to introduce some of the peripheral topics all small business owners will need to deal with when selling a business and I suspect almost without exception, areas we would prefer not to have to deal with as these topics are generally not part of our core competency. The topics I am referring to include tax planning and the tax consequences when selling a business, legal items including making sure all sellers are on board with the sale as well as the legal documents used in the sale, plus accounting and finance issues. In this section we also look at business valuations and their variations as well as the different professional services available for hire including those of a business broker.

Tax Planning

As much as we hate to admit it, taxes are important. Our world wouldn't turn without them and while we may think the IRS is "out to get us," they are an act of congress to enforce the tax code.

If you ask any small business owner—let's make that *any business owner*—what is one of the top reasons for owning a business, they will most often say it is because of the money. To maximize the money you make (and conversely minimize the amount you lose or pay in taxes) you choose a legal entity to get the most legal protection, but one that allows you to pays the least in taxes.

Now that you are thinking about selling your privately held business, it is the right time to find out more and to ask questions about the tax implications to you if it sells. Most business owners DO NOT do this as they either don't have enough time, don't know who or what to ask, don't want to know because they are concerned the price they pay for the advice will be greater than the return or a combination of any and all of these. And that's the point here. This is a reminder that this is something you need to look into *now*. There's no point in waiting until you have an offer on the table.

Purchase Price Allocation

A related subject that should be discussed with a tax planner is purchase price allocation. Just prior to the business closing escrow, one of the documents that should be completed and one of the negotiation points a seller and buyer need to agree on is the Purchase Price Allocation.

The Purchase Price Allocation is an agreement between the buyer and the seller not only on the total price of the business, but how much is being allocated for tax purposes to values such as goodwill, covenant not to compete, trade name, leasehold improvements and fixtures, furniture and equipment. This tax allocation has tax implications for both the buyer and seller and is another negotiation in the transaction. The allocation must be written and agreed to by both parties as the allocation is reported to the IRS.

Sources of additional information include:

http://www.irs.gov
http://moneycentral.msn.com/tax/workshop/welcome.asp
http://www.entrepreneur.com/tax
http://www.smartmoney.com/tax
http://www.fool.com/taxes/taxcenter/taxcenter.htm

Legal Planning

I am not an attorney and therefore cannot provide legal advice. My suggestion is that if you need legal advice, please make sure you get it and do all you can to get it from a qualified source. This really applies whether you need legal, accounting, tax or financial planning services. Yes, it does cost money, but the price you pay should save you so much more in either correcting a mistake or spending the time recovering from a self-inflicted problem that now needs professional help to resolve.

Some common legal areas to understand include the following:

Stock Sale vs. Asset Sale

When you sell your business you may have two choices. If you are operating your business as a Sole Proprietor, Limited Liability Company (LLC) or Partnership, you can only sell the assets of your business. If your legal entity that holds the assets of the business is a C-Corporation or S-Corporation, then you could have the option of selling the assets of the business or the stock (or shares) of the corporation if the buyer is also agreeable.

Stock Sales are not very common in privately held companies. However the following table from Pratt's Stats suggests otherwise.

Total Transactions	Sales Range $	Stock Sales	% of Stock Sales
3658	0 – 1,000,000	422	11.5
937	1,000,001 – 2,000,000	268	28.6
1042	2,000,001 – 5,000,000	499	47.9
799	5,000,001 – 10,000,000	497	62.2
695	10,000,001 – 20,000,000	435	62.8

Make sure an Asset Purchase Agreement or Stock Sale is prepared by a qualified party. There is too much at stake for something not being done correctly.

Advantages of a Stock Sale vs. Asset Sale

Buyer:
1. The buyer doesn't pay sales tax on fixtures and equipment where states have this tax.
2. The current contracts in place with the existing customers, employees and suppliers continue so there is no need to negotiate all over again.
3. No disruption to Accounts Receivable or Accounts Payable - just continue business as usual.
4. In about half the transactions, a lower purchase price.
5. Working capital is part of the transaction and already in place.

Seller:
1. No need for the seller to collect the accounts receivable.
2. Seller has sold his legal responsibilities of the corporation.
3. Potential upside on taxes.

Letter of Intent

The use of a Letter of Intent normally happens in more sophisticated transactions. If the deal is straight forward and the seller and buyer seem to be in agreement on the terms of the deal, a Stock Purchase Agreement or Asset Purchase Agreement can be written by a qualified agent. However, if the deal is complex and both parties want to see if there is common agreement on most if not all the terms of a deal, a Letter of Intent allows one party to make a non-binding offer to get feedback from the other party.

Just to be confusing, some parts of the Letter of Intent can be binding. For example, confidentiality clauses or a "no-shop" agreement that indicates the other party will not negotiate with any other party while the Letter of Intent is in play. Letters of Intent are best written and presented by an agent so discussions and counter discussions can take place without the principals in the transaction getting frustrated with each other.

Agency

If you are planning on hiring the services of a professional to assist you in selling your business, you will need to be clear on the role that person plays and what you can expect from them under the law, or more specifically, the area of commercial law and how it deals with contractual relationships. This area of the law is called Agency and allows a party called the Principal to appoint an Agent. For example, if you are the seller of the business, you are the Principal and would hire an agent to act for you and create legal relationship with a third party.

There are generally three broad classes of agents:

- ✓ A **Universal Agent** acts for the Principal for an extended period of time and with broad responsibilities under, for example, a Power of Attorney. A good example is an attorney.
- ✓ **General Agents** are given responsibility for an extended period of time for specific purposes. Examples could include an insurance company or a company managing a person's medical responsibility because they were unable to do it themselves.
- ✓ **Special Agents** are generally hired for a specific transaction or for multiple transactions but for a short period of time. Examples would include a business broker or business intermediary.

Business Broker

A lot of owners hire a business broker or business intermediary to assist in selling their business. For the contract between the owner or the Principal to be valid, a Listing or Representation Agreement must be signed and executed by both parties.

Listing or Representation Agreements come in the following types:

1. **Sole and Exclusive** (also called Exclusive Right to Sell)
This agreement is between the Principal and a broker and gives the broker the right to a commission even if the seller introduces the buyer to the transaction.

2. **Exclusive Agency**
This agreement is between the Principal and one broker but only allows the broker to be paid a commission if he/she introduces the buyer to the transaction. If the seller brings the buyer then the broker is not paid a commission.

3. **Open Listing**
This agreement allows the Principal to hire as many brokers as they chose with their liability to only pay a commission to the broker that introduces the buyer and closes the transaction.

4. **Single Party**
This agreement is between the Principal and the broker and allows the broker to earn a commission if he/she introduces a specific buyer that closes the transaction. That is, the broker will have a relationship with a specific buyer that has asked the broker to represent them and this party is who the broker wants to introduce to the seller.

5. Consultants

With all the complexities of owning and running a business it is not unusual for business owners to have a business coach or consultant they work with on a regular basis. Selling a business does not generally happen quickly. According to the California Association of Business Brokers, it is taking an average of 6.6 months to sell a business—if it sells. Having a consultant to provide advice through the process is a great benefit, especially if the transaction has complications.

Potential Roadblocks

Leases

The number one reason a business does not sell is because of the lease. The terms and conditions of the existing lease or the problems created trying to negotiate a lease with the landlord can cause the deal to fall apart.

When selling a business you have to agree to all the details with the buyer for the deal to go through. When a lease is involved, however, by virtue of the terms and conditions in the lease, the landlord has the right to approve the buyer.

Most leases are very complex. They are generally written by attorneys or parties that are very experienced with doing this. Most sellers do not have a lot of training or experience when reviewing a lease so either pull out your lease early and study it so you have more understanding about it or pay somebody to do this for you.

Licenses and Permits

Most states have laws that control the issuing of licenses for services provided by contractors, the sale or serving of alcohol, handling food in restaurants, guns, night clubs, etc. If your business has a permit or license, now is the time to make contact with the relevant agency to refresh yourself on the rules and conditions. It is important to do this before you receive an offer on your business. Laws change so you want to be current with the latest requirements. Also, get related application or transfer forms to show buyers.

Sources of additional information include:

http://www.nolo.com
http://www.lesi.org
http://www.legalzoom.com
http://www.bizfilings.com
http://public.findlaw.com

Accounting

Some business owners choose to do their own bookkeeping. Nobody is more concerned about the money coming in and going of a business than the owner so doing their own bookkeeping allows them to stay on top of it. With excellent software available at very reasonable prices, this makes this task easier and cost-effective for the seller to manage in-house.

Just as many business owners choose to outsource the accounting to a bookkeeper. This ensures that the financial records are in great shape for handing off at year's end and for preparation and filing of tax returns and other year end reports and statements. Other business owners choose to hire a Certified Public Accountant (CPA) to perform not only the bookkeeping, but provide an analysis and areas to improve the bottom line of the business.

The point is, regardless of how the bookkeeping in the business has been done, these documents will form the core of many data points and decisions about the final selling price of the business including the ability of the buyer to get a loan. If these records are not in good shape, it greatly reduces the chances of selling the business. Consider this—if a buyer is looking at two businesses and one business has poor financial records, then the buyer will go no further. It is as simple as that.

Action Item

If your financial records are not in good shape and you are thinking about selling your business, I suggest you get professional assistance. A business requires at least a 12 month period of financial records for a buyer to feel comfortable with the records and have any chance of getting a loan.

Additional Information/Terms a Buyer May Use

Following are some common questions that the buyer may ask.

Are the accounts done on a cash basis or accrual?

1. Cash-based accounting is one of the two most common methods of accounting. Under this method, income is reported in the tax year actually received and expenses are deducted in the tax year paid.
2. Accrual-based accounting is the other most common method of accounting. Under this method, income is reported in the tax year earned, whether or not received, and deductions are claimed in the tax year incurred, whether or not paid.

Have the financial statements been audited?

There are three types of financial statements:

1. Compiled: This means the financial statements/information is provided by the business owner and there has been no review or double checking by a qualified party, such as a CPA, to make sure the entries or financial statements are accurate.
2. Reviewed: This means a qualified party, such as a CPA, has done testing and analysis that provides a reasonable basis that material modification to the financial statements is not required to make the financial statements conform with GAAP or some other comprehensive basis of accounting. Compiled financial statements are no assurance of accuracy whereas reviewed means we are getting there but what we really want is audited.
3. Audited: This means a qualified party, such as a CPA, has done detailed tests on the financial records and transactions in accordance with generally accepted auditing standards such as GAAP. It also means this qualified party is prepared to sign the financial statements to certify (or stake their reputation) to their accuracy.

If the buyer asks if your financial statements have been audited, for most businesses that answer is almost invariably *no*. It makes little sense for a seller to go to the expense of having their books audited. Normally the only other party that has an interest in the performance of the business apart from the owners is the IRS—and they don't require audited financial statements...thankfully.

The following websites offer more information about understanding financial statements in more detail:

http://www.baruch.cuny.edu/tutorials/statements
http://www.studyfinance.com/lessons/finstmt/index.mv
http://www.t-tlaw.com/fin-03.htm
http://www.bizzer.com/images/Financial
http://www.allbusiness.com/accounting-reporting/reports-statements/1307-1.html

Transaction Documents

The sale of any business involves a large number of legal and financial documents. The greater the complexity of the business and its sale, the larger the number of documents. In simple terms, the documents include those used in the normal course of running the business such as Profit and Loss Statements, property lease, Franchise Agreement and business tax returns.

Below is a list of the more common documents broken into three groups.
1. Documents the seller would bring to the transaction
2. Documents the buyer would bring to the transaction
3. Documents needed to be completed during the transaction

This information will allow you to collect the documents you will need and research the ones you are not sure about.

Seller Supplied Documents:

- ✓ Profit and Loss Statements for the last three years
- ✓ Balance Sheets for the last three years
- ✓ Statements of Cash Flow (if available)
- ✓ Tax returns for the last three years
- ✓ Sellers Disclosure
- ✓ List of Fixtures, Furniture & Equipment
- ✓ Confidentiality Agreement
- ✓ Resolutions to Sell
- ✓ State Sales Tax returns (if applicable)
- ✓ State Payroll Tax records (if applicable)
- ✓ List of vendors
- ✓ Confidential Business Review

Buyer Supplied or Completed Documents:

- ✓ Signed Confidentiality Agreement
- ✓ Financial statement to show the buyer has the ability to buy the business or make the down payment they are representing
- ✓ Resume to show any skill specialties (if the seller or lender requires)
- ✓ Credit report to assure the seller that the buyer has the ability to get a loan
- ✓ Buyer's Disclosure Statement

Note: If a business requires a conditional license or permit, for example, a permit that precludes the owner from holding a license if they have a felony conviction, then it would be worth requiring the buyer to make a disclosure so time is not wasted on a transaction that can never close.

Other Documents Used During the Transaction

- ✓ Asset Purchase Agreement or Letter of Intent
- ✓ Counter Offer form
- ✓ Bulk Sale information (if applicable)
- ✓ Inventory final count and value
- ✓ Bill of Sale
- ✓ Landlord Waiver (if applicable)
- ✓ Escrow instructions
- ✓ Asset Purchase Price Allocation (if applicable)
- ✓ Fictitious Name Abandonment form (if applicable)

Sources of additional information include:

www.business.gov
www.findlaw.com
www.lawyers.com
www.copyright.gov
http://www.businesslaw.gov

Financing The Sale

An important topic to consider is the question of seller financing. In general terms, financing can be provided by the seller or the buyer can secure funding from different sources such as family, friends, banks or credit unions. These are not necessarily typical sources of funds for every buyer, but other options include:

- ✓ Cash the buyer has been saving
- ✓ Home equity loan
- ✓ Local banks
- ✓ Small Business Administration (SBA)

Seller Financing

Apart from the sources the buyer has to secure finance, an option often explored is whether or not the seller is prepared to carry some of the financing or carry a note. In some situations, in order to get the deal done it may require a combination of a buyer down payment, funding from a third party and a seller note. The benefits to the seller to consider seller financing include:

- ✓ Helps close the deal
- ✓ Additional profit for the seller
- ✓ Monthly cash flow after the business has closed escrow
- ✓ Tax advantages
- ✓ A better return on their money than in a traditional bank account.
- ✓ "Lifestyle" benefits
- ✓ Estate planning benefits

Seller Financing Formats

Seller financing can happen in a variety of ways:

Secured Notes	Unsecured Notes (not recommended)	Assumption of Seller Guaranteed Credit
Assumption of Capital Leases	Earn Outs	Seller Consigned Inventory
Non-Compete Agreement	Life Insurance	Health Insurance
Notes on Capital Equipment	Employment Agreement	Severance Agreement
Closing Bonus	Real Estate Lease	Family Employment
Fee for Staying on Lease	Fee for Guaranteeing Lease	Royalties
Licenses	Commissions	Signing Bonus

Right to Offset

An important item to know is whether your state recognizes the buyer's right to offset a seller's note if information is not disclosed or a misrepresentation is made. Proper tax planning and professional advice are necessary to make sure all the aspects and the best structure of any finance agreement is explored, fully understood and all contracts are correctly written and executed.

Sources of additional information include:

SBA Loan program:	http://www.sba.gov
Small Business finance:	http://www..vfinance.com
Financial research:	http://www.ww.ibbotson.com
Finance options:	http://www.business.com/Finance.asp
CNN Money:	http://money.cnn.com/index.html
Federal Government Small Business Finance:	http://www.business.gov/guides/finance

Business Valuations

This is an intriguing topic and critical to all owners wanting to sell their business. Interestingly, one of the first questions asked is: *How much is my business worth?* There is a lot of information available on this topic but here are immediate considerations:

1. Beware of the scams
2. Valuations or appraisals could be required for different parts of the business and they are rarely done by the same appraiser as they each have specialized training. For example, valuations could include the business in its own right, the land and the buildings if owned by the business owner, the machinery and equipment and any intangible items such as trademarks, copyrights and/or patents.
3. The result of the valuation could be different even if the appraisal is done by the same appraiser.

Beware of Scams

There is a cottage industry of sales people calling on business owners and selling a business valuation—sometimes with an open listing agreement. These sales people offer to do a valuation of the business generally for a high fee—anywhere from $5,000 to $30,000 and more.

As an inducement to get the fee for the valuation, these sales people offer to take an open listing. This means the owner of the business is free to find their own buyer. However, the sales person offers to advertise and bring qualified buyers (or part of the pitch is that they already have them) and then receive a commission only if the business sells. The business owner thinks this is reasonable for three reasons.

First, the business owner needs a valuation and they are not sure how this done. Second, the sales person only gets paid a commission if the business sells and third, the sales person says he/she has a buyer.

There are two indicators that this is a scam. The first is that the price the business owner pays for the valuation is very high. Second, the sales person suggests their company has a lot of interested buyers and they have a great chance of bringing a qualified buyer to the business owner, when in fact this is highly unlikely.

Some clues that this may not be as good as it seems are that the sales person is either from out of state or they are passing through the area and will not be back for a long period of time. Plus, the sales people tend to use pressure tactics and threats like: "If you are not interested, I will go to your competitor just down the road."

Types of Valuation

Business valuations can be very complex. It is critical for a professional business appraiser to understand the purpose of the valuation.

There are three types of valuations:
1. A Brokers Opinion of Value—Costs from $500 to $1,000 depending on the complexity.
2. A Standard Valuation—Costs from $3,000 to $5,000 depending on the structure of the business, the reason and complexity of the valuation.
3. A Full Appraisal—Costs from $7,500 for complex valuations that do or may involve litigation.

To help understand valuations it is necessary to understand Uniform Standards of Professional Appraisal Practice (USPAP). USPAP sets the generally accepted standards for professional appraisal practices in North America, similar in purpose to GAAP which is used by the accounting profession.

A Brokers Opinion of Value is not USPAP compliant. However, if the purpose of the valuation is to establish a listing price for the business and the methods used to determine the Brokers Opinion of Value are reasonable, then it could be argued that this is all the business owner needs. The final price is decided by the market and the ability to locate a buyer willing to pay the price for which the business sells. Additionally, the cost of a Brokers Opinion of Value is not burdensome and may save you the expense of a Standard Valuation or Full Appraisal.

Purpose of the Valuation

To be a little clearer, it is mentioned above that there are three types of valuations; the Brokers Opinion of Value, a Standard Valuation and a Full Appraisal. The type of valuation to choose would depend on the purpose of the valuation. The Brokers Opinion of Value is mainly used by a business owner to understand the listing price of the business.

A Standard Valuation or a Full Appraisal would be requested depending on the reason for the valuation. If a matter is going to court for litigation, generally a Full Appraisal would be requested so there is a thorough examination of all aspects of the business. The other purposes of a Standard Valuation or Full Appraisal could be:
✓ Establishing the value of a minority owners portion of the business
✓ Agreeing on a value to settle a divorce
✓ Starting or maintaining an employee stock ownership program
✓ Settling a Buy/Sell Agreement
✓ Establish the initial value of the business to start a Buy/Sell Agreement

Valuations are also required by finance companies before they will approve a loan. But the finance companies would order the valuation and define the terms of the valuation. Hence, as I already mentioned, the result of the valuation could be different even if it is done by the same appraiser on the same business because it depends on the purpose of the valuation.

Valuation Methods

Valuations are based on either the Market method, the Cost or Income method or the Asset method— or a combination of any or all of these. Within each method there are different valuation approaches as determined by the appraiser. This may be argued, but for privately held business valuations, the International Business Brokers' Association arrives at the value of a business called the Most Probable Selling Price or MPSP.

The MPSP comes from the Fair Market Value of tangible assets plus intangible assets plus goodwill then plus or minus any other adjustments. Fair Market Value (FMV) is a common standard used by professional appraisers when valuing a business. Business brokers affiliated with the International Business Brokers Association generally use MPSP as the standard. The main difference between MPSP and FMV is that MPSP considers either the buyer or seller or both to be under a compulsion to make a decision and so this affects the final price they are willing to pay or accept. FMV is the amount that the business would change hands between a willing seller and a willing buyer when neither is under compulsion and when both parties have reasonable knowledge of the facts of the business.

Discretionary Earnings

When conducting an appraisal for a business, the basis of the valuation generally comes from determining the Discretionary Earnings the business generates, generally over the last three years of the business operating. Discretionary Earnings has different names including Discretionary Cash Flow (DCF) and Owners Discretionary Earnings.

Explaining Discretionary Earnings is a subject in its own right and too much information for this guide. However, if it is an important subject to you and you would like to understand this topic a little more, section nine demonstrates how Discretionary Earnings are calculated. It also includes a template for you to try and calculate Discretionary Earnings along with a sample to show you how it is done.

Phantom Assets

An interesting question that comes up a lot of the time for business owners and getting their business valued is what is included in the selling price. This may seem totally obvious, but that isn't always the case. Most sellers will say that the price includes the customer list, fixtures, furniture and equipment (FF&E), inventory and vehicles (if applicable). Plus, most sellers believe they have something "unique" that makes their business special and they should therefore be paid extra.

For example, the business is on a street corner, it has 20,000 cars passing it every day, the employees are the best trained and deliver the best service in the county or we have been in business 45 years. The reality is that you have been paid for these unique factors as is currently reflected in your bottom line. The point is that you cannot expect to be paid for it twice and a buyer looking to buy a business will decide what "valuation propositions" are important to them and reflect it in their offer to buy the business.

Some other phantom "value propositions" that sellers want to be paid extra for are shown in the following table.

Seller "Phantom" Assets

Strong local economy	Above average industry ratios	Custom built factory
Strong management team	Loyal customer base	Extensive supplier list
Best reputation for 5 counties	Best delivery system	Location
Best staff in the industry	Growing industry	Low employee turnover
Trade secrets	Licenses	Mailing list
Royalty agreements	Tooling	Name recognition
Backlog	Advertising materials and campaigns	Computer database
Copyrights and Trademarks	Contracts	Engineering drawings
Government programs	Employee manual	Training systems and procedures
Recession proof industry	Technologically advanced equipment	Being in business 60 years

As mentioned earlier, business valuations are complex. You could have five appraisers in the same room and walk out with six opinions and nobody agreeing on which one of them had two opinions. The real purpose of this section on valuations is to ensure that as the owner of a business, when looking to sell your business and establish a listing price, do not over-pay for the valuation or appraisal.

Other Types Of Valuation

The most common valuation needed by business owners is someone to value the entire business. However, other valuations are necessary and generally do not include the same person that does your business valuation. These include:

Commercial Real Estate Valuations

When the owner of the business also owns the land and the buildings, a real estate valuation is necessary. It is common to obtain a value for the business and get an approximate valuation or set of comps on the land and building. A formal appraisal to establish a Fair Market Value for the land and buildings is usually needed prior to closing escrow or in order to have a loan approved for the buyer to make the purchase.

Machinery and Equipment Appraisals

If a business is asset-rich (oil drilling equipment, farm machinery, earth moving equipment, trucks, etc.), it may make sense to have a Machinery and Equipment Appraiser put a value on these assets of the business. Sometimes the true value in the business is the assets and this assessment forms the basis of the business operation and its value.

Intellectual Property Valuations

Sometimes the value of a business may be tied up or hidden in a trademark, patent, trade secret or other form of intellectual property such as a Web domain name or recipes. The first step is to make sure it is clear who owns the intellectual property. The second step is to make sure it can be transferred or sold. If this looks good then the next step is to value the intellectual property.

Sources of additional information include:

Valuation data resources:	http://www.valuationresources.com
Intellectual Property education:	http://www.royaltysource.com/education.html
Intellectual Property:	http://www.uspto.gov
Business Valuation Resources:	http://www.bvresources.com
Institute of Business Appraisals:	http://www.go-iba.org/event_links.asp

Hiring Professionals

One of the decisions that needs to be made is what help, if any, should you get to sell your business. I suggest that you assemble a primary team and a secondary team. Your primary team should include your immediate family and/or closest friends while your secondary team includes professionals you hire for their skill and expertise. Though you should be careful not to have too many members on either team as it becomes unwieldy, time consuming and often, expensive.

A lot of business sellers are reluctant to hire professionals. Reasons include their belief that the cost is too high, the professional doesn't know as much about their business as they do, the seller cannot readily find the right person or someone they know used that service and had a bad experience.

If the right professional is hired for the right reason, the value they bring should far outweigh their cost. This value will be in saving the seller time, increasing the price the seller gets in the event that the business sells, bringing expertise to solve a problem or providing an impartial perspective to an unexpected situation.

In section three we will look at the process to follow to hire these professionals while in section four we will discuss assembling your team. However, here are some thoughts on the professionals you may need to hire, how to find them and most importantly, how to make sure you have the right one on your team.

Accreditation

If you are looking for a professional with a specific skill set, then their accreditation will tell you the education they have obtained for that specialized skill. There are literally hundreds of three and four letter accreditations. To see if that accreditation is what you are looking for, simply do a Google search. Another option is to find their website and read about their education levels so you are comfortable that they have the academic expertise to help you.

Compensation

Is the advisor being compensated by commissions on the sale or are they charging you a fee for a service? Some advisors have a combination where they get a fee for a certain part of their time but also can get commission if they make a sale. Fully understand how they are compensated to make sure it makes sense to you.

Small Business Knowledge and Experience

Going to college and reading and passing the courses and networking with small business owners is nice. However, where the rubber hits the road, it is experience that counts. Look for someone with experience who understands the dynamics, pressures, stresses and responsibilities that business ownership demands. This should be one of the foremost skills you need from any small business advisor. The best way of finding that person probably comes from networking with other small business owners who have "been there and done that."

Expert Network

A good advisor should have a strong network of accountants, attorneys, consultants, appraisers, lenders and other specialists they can refer to you. Referrals are the main stay of most advisors because the work they do often permeates into other disciplines. Their work is therefore exposed to other professionals that get to know not only the advisor's professional work, but also their reputation.

Goal and Style Synergy

You may meet many advisors but what you are looking for is *the right one*. If honesty and trust are important to you, that will be the type of advisor that will work best for you. Similarly, as you work with an advisor you will build a relationship, and so it is important the person you are dealing with understands what you are about and is able to communicate clearly. As mentioned earlier, if the advisor just wants to use buzzwords and jargon to inflate their importance, then that may not be the type of advisor you want working with you.

Reputation and References

As a business owner you value word of mouth and your reputation. It is therefore rewarding to thank professionals you think highly of by using their services again or referring them to somebody you know that needs that same service. However, a lot of the work the advisors do is highly confidential so they have to be careful when handing out references. If a referral is given unsolicited from a "happy customer" that you know professionally, that should give you encouragement to further inquire about using that professional's services.

Accountant/Tax Advisor

There are three types of accounting professionals a business owner may consider hiring to assist with the sale of the business. These are a Certified Public Accountant (CPA), tax attorney or a personal financial planner. The option chosen will likely come down to cost, the specifics of the seller's situation including the complexity of the business being sold and the advice needed, the tax advice implications, and the existing relationships the seller has with any of these professionals.

The above list is not to suggest that others can't assist. For example, there are many street-wise and highly skilled bookkeepers that may have intimate knowledge of a business and can readily advise a seller. However, if the seller is looking for a professional to hire and he/she has no existing relationships, then these are the professionals to consider.

Resources for Locating CPAs:
American Institute of Certified Public Accountants   http://www.aicpa.org
Thomas Financial   http://www.thomasonfinancial.com

Tax Attorneys:
Lawyers.com   http://www.lawyers.com
National Association of Enrolled Agents   http://www.naea.org/MemberPortal
Findlaw.com   http://www.findlaw.com

Sources of additional information include:
National Association of Financial and Estate Planners   http://www.nafep.com/index.html
Risk Management Association   http://www.rmahq.org/RMA
Walker Advisory Associates   http://www.waa-online.com/new/waaonline

---

A Word of Caution

It is not unusual for accountants, attorneys and tax advisors to be <u>deal killers</u>. Their training and core competency is to protect and therefore advise their clients about minimizing financial, legal and tax risks. Similarly, they don't want to give "risky" advice—such as encouraging you to accept an offer—and lose a customer or generate negative word of mouth because something went wrong in the deal.

Selling a business does come with risk. It is therefore not unusual for an accountant, attorney and/or tax agent to offer conservative advice as they are not comfortable with a deal point or their "risk" barometer discourages the seller (or buyer) from moving forward with the transaction.

Bottom line: Make sure you have people on your team who will give you good advice on how best to sell your business—not just to protect you from a mistake they feel is important to them.

Appraiser

There are many types of appraisers and they belong to different organizations depending on which specialty the practitioner enjoys. All appraisal standards flow from the Uniform Standards of Professional Appraisal, therefore look for an appraiser whose organization is centered in USPAP. A business seller should be able to find an appraiser for the service they need from the following categories, though you can search the Internet if your need is not met.

Business Appraiser

There are many designations for different type of business appraisers. The following Web links will take you to the different organizations that will allow you to search for a local member in your area.

International Business Brokers Association	http://www.ibba.org
Institute of Business Appraisals	http://www.go-iba.org
National Association of Certified Valuation Analysts	http://www.nacva.com

Commercial Real Estate Appraiser

There are also many designations for different types of real estate appraisers. The following Web links will allow you to search for a local member in your area.

The Appraisal Institute   http://www.appraisalinstitute.org
Commercial Real Estate Institute
            http://www.ccim.com/members/professional_directory_public.html
National Association of Real Estate Appraisers   http://narea-assoc.org/about.php

Machinery and Equipment Appraiser

The main designation is the Certified Machinery and Equipment Appraiser (CMEA) and this is managed by the National Builders and Business Institute in Wichita, Kansas.

National Equipment Business Brokers Institute   http://www.nebbi.org

Intellectual Property Appraiser

Willamette Management Associates   http://www.willamette.com/index.html

Attorney

Just as there are specialists in finance and accounting due to the breadth of the subject, so too are their experts in the different fields of law. It is important that you find an attorney that specializes in the specific area of law you need.

The American Bar Association: http://www.abanet.org
Your state's Bar Association: http://www.abanet.org/barserv/stlobar.html

Sources of additional information include:
http://www.abanet.org/public.html
http://www.legalzoom.com

Business Broker

Business brokers, also known as business Intermediaries, provide a range of services and have two primary benefits. The first is allowing the owner of the business to continue doing what they do best (run the business) while the broker finds a buyer. Second, the broker acts as a neutral party that understands the business and can be a conduit between the seller and buyer, listening and processing questions and keeping things moving forward.

Other benefits include:
- ✓ Provide a Brokers Opinion of Value for a suggested listing price for the business
- ✓ Handle and coordinate buyer prospecting
- ✓ Bring a higher sale price
- ✓ Negotiate all aspects of the transaction—and often there are many negotiations within a negotiation
- ✓ Professional marketing program to reach more potential buyers
- ✓ Facilitate the closing process
- ✓ Assist each party's support team

On the next page is a checklist of items a qualified business broker should be able to provide. In some states a business broker is required to hold a license as they are facilitating the sale of personal property and sometimes real property; so if it's required make sure it is in place.

One of the most important ingredients a seller needs when looking for a broker is trust. If you don't feel the broker has your best interests at heart, then look for another one.

The International Business Brokers Association (IBBA) is a global organization and has the largest membership of business brokers in the United States. It provides a forum for the industry including education standards for business brokers to obtain accreditation with the designation of Certification of Business Intermediary (CBI).

Typical Checklist Used By A Business Broker

Valuing the Business
- ✓ Brokers Opinion of Value with Most Probable Selling Price
- ✓ Recasting the financial statements to support Brokers Opinion of Value
- ✓ Review by a certified business intermediary

Preparing to Sell
- ✓ Coordinating a furniture, fixtures & equipment list
- ✓ Lease summary
- ✓ Federal tax returns (3 years)
- ✓ Profit and loss statements (3 years)
- ✓ Franchise agreement summary
- ✓ Corporate or LLC resolution
- ✓ List of competitors

Packaging the Business
- ✓ Executive summary
- ✓ Internet listing summary
- ✓ Confidential Business Review

Marketing the Business
- ✓ Marketing plan preparation
- ✓ Ad composition
- ✓ Direct mail campaign, if appropriate
- ✓ Newspaper advertising
- ✓ Internet advertising
- ✓ Other business opportunity sites
- ✓ Search buyer database
- ✓ Advertising to business intermediaries with California Association of Business Brokers and International Business Brokers Association

Qualifying the Buyer Prospects
- ✓ Non-Disclosure Agreement
- ✓ Buyer financial statement
- ✓ Buyer interview and profile
- ✓ Credit report, if applicable

Showing and Negotiating
- ✓ Preliminary discussions/suitability
- ✓ Show business
- ✓ Prepare seller for buyer meeting
- ✓ Assist in deal negotiation

Preparing the Purchase Agreement
- ✓ Draft Asset Purchase Agreement
- ✓ Draft addendums
- ✓ Create transaction timelines
- ✓ Create due diligence list
- ✓ Seller's Promissory Note terms, if applicable
- ✓ Draft counter offer, if required

Conducting Due Diligence
- ✓ Checklist development and contingency sign-off
- ✓ Compilation of due diligence materials and book
- ✓ Due diligence assistance

Assist in Finding Financing
- ✓ SBA loan process, if applicable
- ✓ Preliminary interview
- ✓ Pre-qualifications of buyer
- ✓ Mini business plan and projection
- ✓ Full application preparation
- ✓ Dealing with preferred lender officer
- ✓ Seller's Promissory Note, if applicable
- ✓ Assisting with escrow company
- ✓ Seller note, if applicable
- ✓ Other third party sources, if applicable

Closing the Transaction
- ✓ Drafting instructions to escrow company
- ✓ Preparing document package for escrow company
- ✓ Obtaining franchisor approval, if applicable
- ✓ Obtaining lease assignment, if applicable
- ✓ Developing orderly turnover plan
- ✓ Drafting Allocation of Purchase Price
- ✓ Negotiating escrow company closing fees
- ✓ Expediting escrow company
- ✓ Closing coordination

Sources of additional information include:

International Business Brokers Association   http://www.ibba.org

There are also a lot of US states with Business Broker Associations including the following:

Arizona Association of Business Brokers, Inc.	http://www.azbba.net
California Association of Business Brokers, Inc	http://www.cabb.org
Colorado Association of Business Intermediaries	http://www.cabisource.org
Business Brokers of Florida	http://www.fbba.com
Carolina-Virginia Business Brokers Association	http://www.cvbba.com
Georgia Association of Business Brokers, Inc	http://www.gabb.org
Mid-Atlantic Business Brokers Association	http://www.mabba.org
Midwest Business Brokers Association	http://www.mbbi.org
Michigan Business Brokers Association	http://www.mbba.org
New England Business Brokers Association	http://www.nebba.com
New York Association of Business Brokers	http://www.nyabb.org
Northwest Association of Business Brokers	http://www.fbba.com/northwest.asp
Ohio Business Brokers Association	http://www.obba.org
Pennsylvania Business Brokers Association	http://www.pennbba.com
Texas Association of Business Brokers	http://www.tabb.org
Washington-Baltimore Business Brokers Association	no web address

Business Consultants

Business Consultants offer specialized services and are especially useful to owners that are thinking of selling but know the business could obtain a higher price if a little Tender Loving Care was applied to it before listing it for sale. Additionally, business consultants have different areas of specialty and may be able to assist owners with some of the following:

- ✓ Cash flow problems
- ✓ Employee/management issues
- ✓ Declining sales and/or profitability
- ✓ Obtaining loans/finance

Sources of additional information include:

Turn Around Management Association	http://www.actp.org
Society of Business Analysts	http://www.societyofbusinessanalysts.com
Institute of Certified Business Counselors	http://www.i-cbc.org
Association of Corporate Growth	http://www.acg.org
International Business Brokers Association	http://www.ibba.org

Personal Financial Planner

Earlier in this section we discussed whether hiring an accountant or tax advisor was necessary. We mentioned that a personal financial planner may be an option that works for some sellers, especially if the planner you are considering hiring is experienced in advising on financial statements. Specific skills or characteristics to consider when looking for a personal financial planner include the following:

Accreditation

There are literally dozens of three and four letter accreditations. These include specializations such as CLU (Chartered Life Underwriter) for life insurance or QPA (Qualified Pension Administrator) for business retirement and benefit plans. Investment advisors must register with the Securities and Exchange Commission and become RIAs (Registered Investment Advisors). Advisors with more sophisticated training include Certified Financial Planners (CFP) and ChFC (Chartered Financial Consultant).

Compensation

When hiring a financial planner, there are three compensation options available. First, they can be compensated by commissions on the sales of investment and insurance products. Second, they can be fee-based only or third, they can charge you a fee for a service but also can get commissions for products they sell.

Sources of additional information include:

Certified Financial Planner Board of Standards	http://www.cfp.net
Chartered Financial Consultant	http://www.chfc-clu.com

The Perfect Business

The perfect business is one with the following attributes:

1. A reasonable price
2. A reasonable down payment (hopefully about 30% of the full price)
3. Some seller financing
4. Reasonable sales (hopefully increasing each year)
5. Discretionary Earnings of $60,000 per annum or more
6. A compelling reason for sale
7. A desired industry type
8. Good and attractive location (if important for the business type)

More Resources

Books
Small Business Books   http://www.smallbizbooks.com
Amazon   http://www.amazon.com
Borders   http://www.borders.com
Books Online   http://www.booksonline.com

Magazines
Inc. Magazine   http://www.inc.com
Entrepreneur Magazine   http://www.entrepreneur.com
Forbes Magazine   http://www.forbes.com
Business Week   http://www.businessweek.com

General Business Websites
Small Business Administration   http://sba.gov
IRS   http://www.irs.gov
Yahoo Finance   http://finance.yahoo.com
MSN Money   http://moneycentral.msn.com/home.asp
Stat-USA   http://www.stat-usa.gov
The Deal   http://www.thedeal.com
The Wall Street Journal   http://online.wsj.com/small-business

Coaching/Knowledge
Business.com   http://www.business.com
Franklin Covey   https://www.franklincoveycoaching.com
The Alternative Board   http://www.tabboards.com
Society of Competitive Intelligence Professionals   http://www.scip.org

Other Resources

Small Business Development Center (SBDC)

The Small Business Development Centers provide management assistance to small businesses. To find your local SBDC office, check here: http://sbdcnet.org/sbdc.php

SCORE - Service Corp Of Retired Executives (SCORE)

This national organization has local chapters full of experienced business professionals that have "been there, done that" and wish to give back to their local business community by providing a free consultation/mentoring service.

For more information about SCORE: http://www.score.org

To find a local chapter near you: http://www.score.org/explore_score.html

Chambers of Commerce

http://www.uschamber.com

The Learning Annex

http://www.learningannex.com

Twenty Guaranteed Ways to NOT Sell Your Business

1. It is unclear exactly what is being sold.
2. Failure to explain to the buyer the real value in the business opportunity and determine if this meets their business search criteria.
3. Failure to follow through with an interested buyer and keep the process moving forward.
4. Telling the buyer they are incompetent or don't know what they are doing.
5. Selling when you shouldn't.
6. Talking when you shouldn't.
7. Failing to use common sense.
8. Poor communication and not listening.
9. Giving worldly advice on subjects or matters not relevant to the transaction.
10. Failing to get expert advice or assistance when it is required.
11. Assuming you know what the buyer wants.
12. Failing to understand the buyer's objectives and if the business meets their needs.
13. Improper pre-sale planning and failing to be organized.
14. Answering the question before it is asked.
15. Not allowing the buyer to feel some sense of control in the decision making process.
16. Using high-pressure sales tactics.
17. Letting negative ideas or emotions get in the way.
18. Providing incorrect answers to questions.
19. Trying to sell the business to the wrong buyer.
20. Forgetting that buying a business is a stressful situation for the buyer—just as it is for the owner selling an entity they have labored, cherished and worried about over the years.

End Of Chapter Notes

Use this page to write down notes, ideas and other brainstorming for selling your business.

Section Three

Research Selling Your Business

"If we knew what we were doing it wouldn't be research."

Dr. Albert Einstein

Introduction

Sections one and two cover a lot of the basic terms and concepts when selling a privately held business. The focus of section thee is three-fold. First, it is to look specifically at your business to see if you can uncover any areas that need improvement prior to listing it for sale that should return a higher selling price, or in other words, a simple return on investment. Second, develop a plan so you can build a clear direction and strategy to sell the business. Third, identify any professionals you may want to hire to help with the sale and determine what you can expect those professionals to provide. This will lead you to the ultimate goal of successfully selling your business for the best price with as little stress and frustration as possible.

Just a Reminder

This is a workbook. It is meant for writing, scribbling and making notes. Staple into the pages any notes you take or articles you read. It requires you making notes, finding, reading and writing questions, along with reminders and inspirations about documents or processes. By the time you finish this section you will have available the information a buyer or professional you hire may need. The remaining sections of this book then capture the flow of the transaction and the best practices to follow.

Now, let's do some research!

Franchises

If you are a franchisee, this is your opportunity to prepare your business and anticipate questions so you have answers available for inquiring buyers. Selling a franchise can add an extra layer of complexity. A buyer normally has to negotiate with the seller and landlord and understand their requirements in order to buy the business. However, when a franchise is involved, the franchisor may have financial requirements, management experience or other requirements that the seller is not concerned about. For example, some of the oil companies that license the use of their brand will not approve the transfer of the business to buyers without industry experience. Some franchisors require the buyer to have an MBA. And so the list goes on.

To get you started, I have proposed some questions to research and consider before selling your franchise. Hopefully the questions I have asked will prompt other questions you want to research. Be sure to jot down your questions in the space on the following page.

List any questions you want to ask your franchisor before listing the business for sale.

Questions and/or Research if Selling a Franchise

Question	Answer/Comment
Re-read your UFOC in case you've forgotten points you need to advise a buyer about.	
When does the current UFOC expire? Are there renewal options and costs?	
Is this the current UFOC or is there a new one?	
Can I get a copy of the new one and if so, from whom?	
Does the buyer work under the new UFOC or the old one?	
Is there a franchise transfer fee? How much? Who pays?	
Is a new buyer required to attend training? If so, how much? How long does the training take? How often?	
Is the buyer required to have training before or after the Change of Possession of the business?	
Are there other costs that need to be disclosed to a buyer?	
When should I advise the Franchisor and who do I notify?	
Does the Franchisor have a preferred selling process I need to understand and/or follow?	
Does the Franchisor have an application form they require the buyer to complete? Do you want a copy to show a buyer?	
Are there names of franchisees you can call to learn from their experience in selling their franchise?	

Tax Planning

It is important to determine if selling your business will create tax problems for you and more importantly, if these are problems you want to look into further. The smaller businesses that are sold may not trigger tax problems when they sell but you don't want to have an offer on the table only to find that you have to pay more tax than needed. Or worse still, you accept the offer and close the sale and find the tax consequences are dire.

Most small business owners don't know the answer to this question; it is simply outside their expertise. I have owned and operated five businesses and I always felt my time and expertise was best spent running my business and paying for professional help as needed. However, tax planning makes good business sense so let's dig in a little deeper.

If you have an accountant or tax advisor, this is the first place to start. They should already know your business and your personal tax situation so you will be a step ahead. If instead you use a bookkeeper, ask them for their thoughts. If you prepare your own financial statements and tax returns, find a professional and spend the money for a one- to two-hour consultation.

Make the most of your investment by preparing for your meeting before you visit the accountant. Following are some considerations:
- ✓ Are you after a short-term or long-term relationship—and what are they offering?
- ✓ What education qualifications do they have?
- ✓ What are the costs?
- ✓ What is their small business expertise?
- ✓ Are you better off looking for an advisor that not only knows small businesses but also the particular industry you work in? For example, if your business is a medical practice, are you better off with a tax advisor that knows that industry and some of the "hidden" tax minimization options?
- ✓ Do they have a code of ethics or belong to any associations that do?
- ✓ Do you know somebody else that has used their services? If not, ask for referrals and visit their website to get more information about them.
- ✓ Can you identify their client base? If so, do you think this is a customer base that is similar to the industry you work in?
- ✓ Would they consider a free initial consultation so you can see if there is a match with the service they provide and what you need?

Finding a Tax Advisor

If you have been doing your own bookkeeping or using the services of a bookkeeper, you want to do some research to find a professional who can advise you on minimizing your tax liability after the business sells. You may also want the advisor to be available if questions come up during the sale that may affect the amount of tax that you pay.

When looking for a tax advisor, consider answering the following questions so you find the right person for you.

1. How complex do you consider your situation and how much advice do you think you need? (Obviously a tough question but I suggest listing questions/topics below so you can research and find the answers in order to hire the right person for the job.)
2. Does the person you currently use to prepare your business financial statements and tax returns have the skill to advise you on selling your business? Often they do not want the responsibility of advising on selling a business because it is outside their core competency.
3. Are you looking for a short-term engagement to get answers to questions as you move through the process of selling the business or a long-term relationship?
4. Certified Public Accountants (CPA) and some attorneys are qualified to offer more complex business and personal financial advice; some are not. A CPA that also has a Certified Financial Planner credential is a great resource.

List the tax planning questions you would like to research before listing the business for sale.

Purchase Price Allocation Reminder

Purchase Price Allocation is important, especially in a sizeable transaction of $500,000 or more. As part of your tax planning with your professional, make sure a discussion includes the Purchase Price Allocation so your tax position is understood and even consider coming up with a draft Purchase Price Allocation. If you list the business for sale and you receive an offer, you can suggest to the buyer how you would like the Purchase Price Allocation to look and negotiate it immediately in the transaction rather than leave it to later and find the deal falls apart because both sides couldn't agree.

Finding a Personal Financial Planner

In addition to a tax planner, you may decide you need a personal financial planner. Section two offers some questions to ask when looking for a financial planner. To find the right person for you, ask your accountant or attorney for recommendations. You can also ask business associates for a referral, check the Yellow Pages under Personal Financial Planner or search the Web for local certified financial planners.

Write down any questions you want to ask a personal financial planner.

Legal Planning

Just as we have given some thought to tax planning, there may be a need to do some legal planning. If you've been trading as a partnership and there are disagreements, there may be a need to understand and resolve outstanding legal issues. I know examples where the partnership wasn't working so the three partners agreed to sell. An offer was made and accepted but then one of the partners didn't think it was high enough and backed out. The deal fell through but four months later the business went back on the market making it almost impossible to sell because the partners would not talk with each other.

Divorce is another very common concern. If the business is being sold, make sure there is no legal impediment to the sale. This includes knowing who owns the assets of the business or just as important, if the spouse is going to contest the ownership. It can be incredibly frustrating to have a willing buyer with an offer only to find out it can't be accepted because the spouse won't sign the offer. One way of resolving this is having a Spouse Consent to Sell resolution signed before listing the business for sale.

When selling a business there can be many legal issues. Sometimes they will not reveal themselves until you are in the transaction. For example, issues with the lease or determining what should and shouldn't be in an agreement to buy and how it should be written.

On the next page is a checklist of some suggested legal questions to research. Below you can note questions you want to research that are specific to your business.

Write any legal issues you want to research before listing the business for sale.

Legal Questions To Research

Are any updates or changes to the legal entity required?	Are any resolutions to sell required from partners, ex-spouses, directors, etc.?
Have you read the lease and made sure it is assumable and there are no "deal killer" clauses?	Does the business have an affiliate or related company they do business with that should be disclosed?
Are key employees willing to stay with a new owner?	Is the employee manual up to date and does it meet current laws?
Are any patents, trademarks and other intellectual property correctly registered?	Have all key contracts been reviewed to make sure they are current or can be sold?
If there is leased equipment, can the leases be assumed and who is the point of contact at the leasing company?	If a lien search is done, will it reveal any issues that can be addressed now?
Does any of the equipment need upgrading or removing?	Does the company have difficulties complying with environmental regulations?
Are there any federal, state or licensing requirements that need to be reviewed?	Are all federal and state taxes up to date?
Is there an accurate estimate of the current value of the inventory? Is a report available?	Are OSHA, health department, fire department, EPA, EDD and IRS requirements up to date?
Are there any notes the buyer needs to assume as part of the deal?	Are the union or employee agreements up to date?
Have I9 forms been filed for all current employees?	Are there any legal or medical claims against the business that should be addressed now?
If the business provides customers with warranties that you expect the buyer to take over and honor, are they up to date and clear?	Is workers' compensation up to date?
Is the business in default of any financial or contractual obligations?	

Business Brokers

Here are some considerations when hiring a business broker:
- ✓ Has business ownership experience.
- ✓ Understands Discretionary Earnings, cash flow and Most Probable Selling Price.
- ✓ Has a local office presence. If your broker is a three-hour drive away, how motivated do you think they will be to meet buyers and bring them to see your business?
- ✓ Willing to co-broker with other business brokers. Co-brokering means the business broker is willing to represent just one party in the transaction while allowing another business broker to represent the other party. Some business brokers want to transact "both ends of the deal."
- ✓ Presents a marketing plan for your business.
- ✓ Check credentials. In many states there is no requirement to become a business broker. Check if the broker is affiliated with the International Business Brokers Association (IBBA) or one of the state associations. If affiliated with the IBBA, see if he/she has the Certified Business Intermediary (CBI) credential.

To find a local business broker, consider the following options:
International Business Brokers Association   http://www.ibba.org

There are also a lot of US States with a Business Broker Association including the following:

Arizona Association of Business Brokers, Inc.	http://www.azbba.net
California Association of Business Brokers, Inc	http://www.cabb.org
Colorado Association of Business Intermediaries	http://www.cabisource.org
Business Brokers of Florida	http://www.fbba.com
Carolina-Virginia Business Brokers Association	http://www.cvbba.com
Georgia Association of Business Brokers, Inc	http://www.gabb.org
Mid-Atlantic Business Brokers Association	http://www.mabba.org
Midwest Business Brokers Association	http://www.mbbi.org
Michigan Business Brokers Association	http://www.mbba.org
New England Business Brokers Association	http://www.nebba.com
New York Association of Business Brokers	http://www.nyabb.org
Northwest Association of Business Brokers	http://www.fbba.com/northwest.asp
Ohio Business Brokers Association	http://www.obba.org
Pennsylvania Business Brokers Association	http://www.pennbba.com
Texas Association of Business Brokers	http://www.tabb.org
Washington-Baltimore Business Brokers Association	no web address

Also, as I am a business broker, you contact me directly or through my site: www.andrew-rogerson.com and I will work with you to find a local broker.

Write down the questions you want to ask when researching business brokers.

Finance The Sale

This is an interesting topic to research as the usual course of events is to find a buyer and then let him worry about getting financing to buy the business. What if you had a source of financing lined up? While much depends on the buyer's down payment, their credit score, their business ownership or management skills, and more, you may still benefit from doing some research.

You could spend a lot of time on this and get knocked back but that also helps you understand the marketability of the business. If you cannot get a loan or you need to change how the business is operating to get one, I think it is well worth finding out earlier rather than later. Otherwise you are looking for a buyer that will pay all cash or you will have to carry a large note.

Following are some options to research:

- ✓ The first place to call to inquire if they do business loans is the current bank you use for the business. They have the history of the business banking and can advise you on whether or not they can assist.
- ✓ Another option is to talk with a business broker to see if they can assist with this. An established and successful business broker will have relationships in the market and know what banks or financial institutions will offer financing for different businesses in different industries or be able to do the research for you to find out.
- ✓ Consider the local, regional and national banks. The key here is finding the right person, which can be challenging. To get contacts at a local bank, open your local yellow pages directory, turn to "Banks" and start dialing.
- ✓ Check with your industry trade association to see if they have any contacts.
- ✓ Talk to somebody you know that sold their business and see if they can guide you.
- ✓ The Small Business Administration offers some excellent programs. More details are available on their website: http://www.sba.gov/index.html.

Seller Finance

It is not common for a business to sell for all cash unless the asking price is below $100,000. When it is below this figure it is difficult to find a financial institution interested in underwriting the loan due to all the paperwork and due diligence. Most sellers are reluctant to carry all the financing as they figure the risk involved is too high. It doesn't often make sense to sell the business and let a buyer keep the profit and potentially fail, destroying the business and therefore leaving you with nothing.

Financial institutions like the mix of a buyer down payment with some seller financing. This combination causes them to look more favorably at offering a deal because everyone has "skin in the game."

The research required at this point is twofold.

First, talk with your financial or tax advisor about the implications of carrying the financing. There are tax benefits to the seller as the payments to you are only taxed when they are received. Second, research and understand the risk that goes with seller financing so you know if this is something you would be prepared to consider.

Remember, like any other aspect of the sale, seller financing is a negotiation. The buyer may be asking for seller financing just to see the seller reaction. If the seller says it is out of the question, the buyer may be concerned that the seller is hiding something.

Some questions/responses to give to a buyer that wants seller finance include:

- ✓ What experience do you have running this type of business?
- ✓ How much down payment do you plan on providing?
- ✓ Do you have sources of funds available elsewhere?
- ✓ Please provide your resume and a copy of your credit score I will give it some consideration.

Write down any questions you want to ask a buyer as you consider providing some amount of seller financing.

Research By Interview

When preparing your business for sale, there are two groups of people that you will interview: people who have previously sold a business and your competitors.

Owners that Have Sold a Business

To gain some knowledge about the process of selling your business, consider talking with business owners you know that have been through the process of selling. Interviewing three business owners that have sold is a good number but you can make it more or less—that final decision is yours.

Ideally you should try to find one person that worked in your industry, though it is not mandatory unless you work in a specialized industry. For example, a doctor or physical therapist will almost invariably come from your industry—although I have heard of buyers wanting to purchase a doctor's practice without the training. We live in an interesting world.

Complete the template below by writing down as many questions you feel are relevant. To make the questions less intrusive, put them in order of easy questions to hardest and what's important to you. Start by asking the easy questions first so the person you are interviewing is not too uncomfortable and is more relaxed to answer your more difficult questions.

Write down the questions to ask someone who has sold their business.

Ask and get answers to the following questions – First Seller:

Very briefly, what was your business, and how many employees did you have?
How long did it take to sell the business from the time you had the thought to getting it sold?
Did you sell the business yourself or hire somebody to help you with it?
What three things were the hardest parts of the process?
What do you think are the most important skills or ingredients needed to get the job done?
What would you do differently next time and why?
What would you not do again the next time you decide to sell?

Ask and get answers to the following questions – Second Seller:

Very briefly, what was your business, and how many employees did you have?
How long did it take to sell the business from the time you had the thought to getting it sold?
Did you sell the business yourself or hire somebody to help you with it?
What three things were the hardest parts of the process?
What do you think are the most important skills or ingredients needed to get the job done?
What would you do differently next time and why?
What would you not do again the next time you decide to sell?

Ask and get answers to the following questions – Third Seller:

Very briefly, what was your business, and how many employees did you have?
How long did it take to sell the business from the time you had the thought to getting it sold?
Did you sell the business yourself or hire somebody to help you with it?
What three things were the hardest parts of the process?
What do you think are the most important skills or ingredients needed to get the job done?
What would you do differently next time and why?
What would you not do again the next time you decide to sell?

Competitors

When planning to purchase a new TV or major appliance, you check out prices and deals to make sure you have the best one. Now that you are planning to sell your business, it's a good idea to research your top three main competitors for the following reasons:

1. To see how your business compares in case you need to make changes to your business.
2. Check prices to make sure you are competitive.
3. Check the appearance of their business compared to yours in case you will get a higher price by sprucing up the place.
4. Your buyers will be doing it so you will be better prepared in case the buyer makes a claim that isn't true. You can also demonstrate to the buyer that you understand your competition and can successfully beat the competition because you know how much better your business is.

Make a list of questions below and then without identifying yourself, contact each of your competitors.

Write down questions to ask your competitors so you are better prepared when talking to a potential buyer.

Review Your Options

These next two pieces of research are designed to provide you with a snapshot of where you are, highlight any areas you'd like to work on to improve the business and be fully prepared for the next steps of listing and selling the business. The first piece is a quick and dirty SWOT analysis. A SWOT analysis looks at Strengths, Weaknesses, Opportunity and Threats.

The second piece is something I call a Reality Check. Its purpose is to allow you some time to pause, look at all the data you've collected and analyzed so far and make that final decision that the business is ready for selling as best you can determine.

SWOT Analysis

A SWOT Analysis helps you identify strengths, weaknesses, opportunities or threats to selling the business. This allows you to decide whether or not to move forward with the listing of the business for sale or where you are in the process in case there are issues to resolve.

Strengths will increase the selling price while weaknesses and threats will reduce the price. Opportunities can go either way. As the seller you can elect to take the opportunities and execute them to add value to the business and therefore increase the price you will get for the business. Alternatively, you can share them with a buyer so the buyer takes advantage of them as one of their motivating factors to buy your business.

Use some of the prompts below and place them in one of the boxes— strength, weakness, opportunity or threat. Make sure you add your own depending on what you think is important in relation to the industry and the business you are in.

Once you've completed the exercise, consider looking at the items in the threat box and decide if you want to work on them before trying to sell the business. Again, make sure you brainstorm other "deal points" and place them in one of the boxes so you can do a final review and take any further action you deem necessary.

Considerations for Your SWOT Analysis
- ✓ State of the local economy
- ✓ Industry - growing or contracting?
- ✓ Business - growing or contracting?
- ✓ Interest rates - declining or increasing?
- ✓ Is yours an interest rate-sensitive business?
- ✓ Lease - in line with market and with renewal options?
- ✓ Owner - hands on with the management of the business?
- ✓ Trained management if the owner leaves?
- ✓ Employees - is turnover above or below market average?

✓ Employees - regular training program in place?
✓ Operations manual - does the business have one?
✓ Financial statements - well maintained or needing attention?
✓ Customer base - increasing or decreasing?
✓ Taxes paid in full?
✓ Inventory level - above or below industry average?
✓ Appearance of the business?
✓ Location of business?
✓ If a franchise - good or bad public image?

Strength	Weakness
Opportunity	Threat

Reality Check

Now is your opportunity to sit back and look through the previous sections to review your notes and re-read what you have done to date. The next step is then to decide your best course of action.

The table below suggests some options with additional lines for you to add other options/ideas. Put a score of 1 to 10 in the right hand column next to each option. The more you like the idea, the higher the score. After you assign all scores, discard the lower scores and focus on the higher scores to make your final decision on your next steps...and then take action.

Option	Score
Do nothing – continue operating the business as is	
Give the business away	
Sell to a family member or friend	
Close the business down and go and get a job	
Find a buyer for the business	

Other Options

If your reality check suggests the business is not yet ready to list for sale as it is not at it is optimum or needs a lot of work before getting to a saleable position, consider some other options. These could include:

1. Bringing in a partner
2. Selling to employees
3. Talking with your trade association to see if they have help options available
4. There are plenty of organizations available to help you including SCORE, the Small Business Development Centers and TAB. Refer back to section one for contact information.
5. If your reality check is that the business is upside down, that is, the business is not generating enough cash flow for you to keep the doors open, consider getting help from the Turnaround Management Association: http://www.actp.org.

Write down any strategic options you are considering for further reflection and research.

8 Tips for a Fast Sale

1. Have a reasonable listing price.
2. Be prepared to negotiate.
3. Have readily available a folder of information for a qualified buyer.
4. Run the business as usual.
5. Make sure the business presents well—give it a "spit and polish."
6. Get a current snapshot of the business financials and keep them up to date.
7. Put together a current list of Fixtures, Furniture and Equipment (FF&E).
8. Consider counting all inventories so the value is known. This helps the buyer   understand the final purchase price.

What's Great About My Business!

Your business is unique. This is especially true to you as you have worked it, loved it and lived it. So, what gets you out of bed every morning to tackle your day and go to work in your business and to make a difference? Make a note in the table below of the items that are important to you so you can mention these to a potential buyer as an ice breaker. These items will be of interest to buyers as part of their decision-making process.

If you cannot think of at least three reasons you love your business, then I'd consider closing down the business rather than selling it. ☺

	Highlights	Why
1		
2		
3		
4		
5		
6		
7		
8		
9		
10		

Summary

The goal of sections one through three have been to provide as much background information and structure as possible when considering selling your business. If you decide to move forward and list the business for sale, sections four through eight will provide a step-by-step breakdown of that process.

End Of Chapter Notes

Use this page to write down notes, ideas and other brainstorming for selling your business.

Section Four

Planning

"*The short-term plan, then, is an operative plan of defining goals in writing and clearly indicating how these goals are to be carried out ...*"

American Management

Introduction

Sections one and two of this guide provides some background information about selling a business. Section three allows you to research and prepare your business for sale. The goal of sections four through eight is to provide a systematic approach to selling a business to enhance the chances of success at the best price. This is the model I use as a business broker and corresponds to the methods endorsed by the International Business Brokers Association and the California Association of Business Brokers—and I am a member of both of these organizations.

Assemble Your Team

The first step is to bring together the team you need to help you sell your business as quickly as possible for the best price. My suggestion is to establish a primary and a secondary team.

Your primary team should consist of those with whom you have a long term relationship. These are people who you can turn to for emotional support as well as those who will give you honest answers to tough questions. The obvious place to look for this kind of support is your family and friends or those in your Circle of Influence that have no conflicts of interest about whether or not your business sells. You may have already identified these team members as you followed the processes you in sections two and three.

The secondary team should consist of those you either hire for their expertise and/or those you want to turn to for specific advice as you move through the transaction. In deciding who these people should be, take into consideration:
1. The skills they bring; you don't want someone with the same skill set if it clashes with your own.
2. A skill set that compliments your own skills and that you believe you are lacking.
3. The amount of time they have to help you and whether they will be readily available.
4. The costs involved in hiring the experts you need.

Keep both your primary and secondary teams as small as possible. The more people on the team, the slower the decision making process. This is due to the fact that everybody needs to be consulted and kept informed. Resist bringing in any extra "passengers" unless they have a skill you need. Excess team members can waste time, create distractions or be unavailable when you need them in a hurry.

If your business is a partnership, consider each person having their own primary team and make sure that all partners agree on who should be part of the secondary team. You don't want cheerleaders on your team; you want business people.

Use the following chart to write down the names of primary and secondary people you need for your team.

NOTE:
When selling a business it is critical that the owner stay focused on business as usual. Selling a business is not a quick process. If you have been the day-to-day manager of your business, you must continue in that role so the business stays at it is current level. Often when the owner decides to sell, he/she fails to keep up with the tasks that make the business successful. When sales start to slip and the buyer sees the business deteriorating, the buyer ultimately backs away from making an offer or closing the deal. Selling a business can be a full time job—hence the reason so many owners outsource the process.

Primary Team Members	Secondary Team Members

Once you build your team, try to avoid changing it.

According to the California Association of Business Brokers, it takes 6.6 months to sell a business—if it sells. During a lot of that time, very little happens. However, when it does, there are multiple decisions to make. If you have to educate a new advisor, then bad decisions can ensue as the advisors may not be aware of all the nuances.

Plan For Selling

It is important to understand that there are many steps throughout the process of selling your business and they are often inter-related. As they say, experience is the best teacher. However, keep in mind the following:

- ✓ Stay focused on what's important to you since you cannot have it all.
- ✓ Reach agreement on what's just been discussed.
- ✓ Reach agreement on the next steps.
- ✓ Reach agreement on who is responsible for those next steps.
- ✓ Reach agreement on the next meeting to review what has transpired and to discuss and plan the next steps.

Step One

There is no question that selling a business requires a huge undertaking both financially and emotionally. In addition, it includes a certain amount of risk which can evolve into a large amount of risk if not managed correctly. The financial and emotional undertakings are straightforward but there are many risks that need to be identified and managed. Start by considering the following:

- ✓ Who should be told and at what stage of the process?
- ✓ If confidentiality is important, what do you say to people you don't want to know that you are selling?
- ✓ What help do you need?
- ✓ How do you sell the business?

The first task is to identify who needs to be told, when, how and by whom. This is important as it is normal to give an immediate reply when a question is asked and you should be prepared. For example, if somebody asked you if your business was for sale, your answer would vary depending if the question was posed by a family member, friend, customer, supplier, your family attorney, or a supplier that you owed money etc.

An "elevator speech" is a prepared response you give when someone asks about your business. You may be surprised to know that you should prepare an "elevator speech" for everyone—including your family.

I recently had a transaction where a buyer was in a hair salon and waiting for her appointment. There was an unknown customer sitting next to her and so the two struck up a conversation. After a short time the conversation moved to the unknown customer telling my buyer about her sister's business for sale and how much the price kept being reduced. The bottom line is that the buyer hired me to broker the business for her and paid about a quarter of what it was worth. So family members do need to be told what they can and cannot say.

The next page has space for you to write the answer you would like to give to the different groups of people that may ask you if your business is for sale. Work out the answer or "elevator speech" you would like to use so you are prepared when the question arises. And make sure the answers you give are truthful and honest; as how you respond is a clue in itself and an opportunity because the buyer you are looking for may be right in front of you.

Write your "elevator speech" for your family members.
Write an "elevator speech" for your customers in case they hear the business is for sale.
Write your "elevator speech" for your suppliers in case they hear the business is for sale.
Write your "elevator speech" for your employees in case they hear the business may be for sale.
Write your "elevator speech" for a competitor in case they hear the business is for sale.
Write your "elevator speech" for potential buyers or the buyer's business broker.

Step Two

Be sure to review all the legal items you uncovered in section three and make sure they are resolved. Use the template below to refresh yourself on these items and take the appropriate action that you feel is necessary. This could include getting any conditions or agreements in place prior to the business being sold. For example, you may need a Consent to Sell form signed by your spouse or your Partnership Agreement may have special terms and conditions for a sale. Conditions reduce the number of eligible buyers, hence the importance of identifying these in detail.

Write down any legal checks you feel are necessary prior to listing the business for sale.

Step Three

Make a clear and final determination about exactly what is being sold. Too many sellers put a business on the market with what I call an "asterisk" next to it. This means that the seller advertises the price and what's included but then indicates that certain items are negotiable. This may sound reasonable but it simply confuses the buyer and can lead to the buyer walking away.

Almost without exception, the buyer wants to include everything because they want the business to be as turn-key as possible. I suggest including everything the business needs to be turn-key. Then let the buyer make an offer they think is reasonable and determine what they do and do not want to include. This is preferable to a seller saying "I won't sell the business for anything less," which simply turns buyers away.

Finally, if something isn't part of the sale, take it out of the business before the buyer sees it and decides they really want it. And be careful—you cannot remove an income producing asset and then expect to get the same price that was determined in your business valuation.

Step Four

On the following two pages are checklists. The first checklist details some suggested items to inspect in your business. This is especially important if your business is a retail location or other leased premises that the buyer will acquire as part of the purchase. This exercise helps you assess the visual appeal of each item on the list and gives you a chance to address any issues that might potentially discourage a buyer. You would go through a similar exercise if you were selling your home.

The second checklist suggests tasks to verify that the business is in order and ready to receive potential buyer inquiries. Both checklists have additional space for you to add your own items as they relate to your business.

---

8 Questions A Buyer May Ask

1. Why is the owner selling?
2. How much is the down payment?
3. In what way is this business unique, special or different?
4. How can the business grow?
5. How much income can the new owner expect? (Be careful how you answer as you don't want to give guarantees.)
6. Will the seller carry any financing?
7. Will the owner stay and work with the buyer?
8. Are there any surprises the new owner will encounter?

Business Pre-Listing Assessment Report

Description	Completion Date
Front doors	
Front signage	
Front footpath	
Fire hazards	
Walls	
Bathrooms	
Storage areas	
Licenses displayed as required	
Aisles	
Rear signage	
Outside storage area	
Shelving	
Items that need painting	
Items that need repair	
OTHER:	

Other Pre-listing Items To Review

Description	Completion Date
Lease	
UFOC	
Create a list of fixtures, furniture and equipment that are part of the sale	
Check that all machinery and equipment is operational	
Inspect warehouse space to ensure it is clean and tidy—and that all the space is needed	
Make sure all vehicles are all in working order, including state emission tests	
Count the inventory (If you hire a company to do it, keep the report)	
Scrap excess material (if applicable)	
Ensure all legal agreements signed by necessary parties to authorize the sale	
Other Documents:	
Employee handbook up to date	
Employee contracts up to date	
OTHER:	
Financial statements accurate and up to date	
Health permits, business licenses, other licenses up to date	

Gather Your Data

It is essential to gather all necessary information in order for your business to be valued or appraised. As we discussed earlier, there are three types of business valuations:
1. A Brokers Opinion of Value
2. A Standard Valuation
3. A Full Appraisal

You will need to gather the following data in order to have your valuation completed:

✓ The most up to date Profit and Loss statement for the current financial year
✓ Tax returns and Balance Sheets for at least the last three years
✓ Approximate value of inventory and the date it was counted (if inventory is part of the sale)
✓ Number of full-time and part-time employees
✓ A list of fixtures, furniture and equipment
✓ Price of leased equipment including the remaining balance on the lease and the amount of the monthly payments
✓ Monthly lease cost for facility
✓ Lease expiration date and the number of renewal options
✓ The amount of square feet being leased

For a franchise business, you will also need:
✓ The monthly royalty fee
✓ The franchise transfer fee (if applicable

Commercial Real Estate Valuations

If the business includes real property and you are hiring a business broker or a business appraiser to value the business, then they should be able to give you an approximate price for the real property. This will allow you to list the business and then accept an offer for the real property subject to a valuation by a qualified appraiser. The benefit of this method is that an appraisal changes with time so if it takes awhile for the business and real property to sell, another valuation may be required and so the cost of the valuation will be incurred twice. Additionally, if the sale requires third party financing from a bank or other commercial lender, they will require their own valuation at the buyer's expense.

To order a real property appraisal, all you need to provide is the business address. The appraiser will get all necessary documents from public records.

Machinery and Equipment Appraisals

If you need a valuation on assets such as oil drilling equipment, farm machinery, earth moving equipment, trucks, etc., you will need a Machinery and Equipment Appraiser.

The data the appraiser needs for a valuation would normally come from your depreciation schedule. The appraiser would check this list to provide an estimated cost of the valuation.

If a depreciation schedule or a list is not available, the appraiser can evaluate the equipment in person. You will need to provide the year of manufacture, make, model and serial number. The appraiser will also need to know if there is anything special about the equipment, how it works and what it does.

Section one provides resources for locating a certified machinery and equipment appraiser.

Intellectual Property Valuations

Appraising Intellectual Property (IP) involves a different skill set than any of the other forms of valuation. Sources for locating IP appraisers can be found in section one. The appraiser will let you know what data you need to provide to complete the appraisal.

Make a list of any questions you want to ask the appraiser(s).

Recast Your Financial Statements

If you were a business broker performing a valuation on a business, you would take all of the data you've just collected and do a financial analysis that includes recasting to arrive at the Discretionary Earnings of the business. Once the Discretionary Earnings have been established, further research is done to determine the Most Probable Selling Price of the business.

Your goal at this point in the transaction, as the seller of your business and its assets, is to make sure you have identified what is being sold and who to contact to get a valuation. Use the chart below to provide an overview of the contacts you've made and any agreed deadlines.

Task	Company to Contact	Phone Number	Contact Name	Price	Job Completion Time
Business Valuation					
Real Property Valuation					
Machinery & Equipment Valuation					
Intellectual Property Valuation					

Determine Value And Assets For Sale

You have collected the data, you have made contact with appraisers for valuations and now you need to record the results so you can move forward with the next part of the transaction.

Use the chart below to record your results and move on to the next step.

List of Assets for Sale	Valuation

Don't lose money when selling your business.

Here's a true story. A business was for sale including the usual items of goodwill, FF&E and inventory, etc. During the first buyer/seller meeting, the buyer asks what assets were included in the price. At the next meeting, the buyer asked again what assets were in the price and specifically if it included certain items as well as the painting in the front lobby. The seller confirmed the items and painting were included and the following day the buyer made an all-cash offer for the business. After the sale closed and ownership transferred to the buyer, the buyer revealed that the painting was a unique piece of art worth more than the entire value of the business.

Bottom line: Determine what assets go with the sale and their value!

Prepare An Executive Summary

The purpose of an executive summary is to provide interested buyers with a "snapshot" of the business. It is generally a single page and allows a buyer to decide if he/she wishes to take their inquiry further. Before handing over this document, make sure a signed Confidentiality Agreement is in place. A good executive summary includes the following:

Price and Terms Summary:
- ✓ Business price
- ✓ Value of inventory
- ✓ Value of the real estate

Estimated Value:
- ✓ Fixtures and equipment
- ✓ Leasehold improvements
- ✓ Real estate

Operations Summary:
- ✓ Current form of business ownership or legal entity
- ✓ Years established
- ✓ Ownership length of current owner
- ✓ Reason for selling
- ✓ Business trading days and hours
- ✓ Licenses required to run the business

Lease Summary:
- ✓ Total monthly rent
- ✓ Security deposit the buyer is required to pay
- ✓ Approximate square feet being rented
- ✓ Lease expiration date
- ✓ Lease renewal options
- ✓ Parking availability

Staff Information:
- ✓ Number of owners working in the business
- ✓ Hours the owners work on a weekly basis
- ✓ Number of managers
- ✓ The salary of the managers
- ✓ Total payroll and wages being paid
- ✓ Number of employees—full-time and part-time

Summary of Income:
- ✓ Summary for the last three years of gross sales, Cost of Goods Sold, Gross Profit, Expenses and a breakdown of all the seller add-backs to arrive at each years Discretionary Earnings

Prepare A Confidential Business Review

A Confidential Business Review (CBR) provides an in-depth presentation of the business to qualified buyers. It is the document that puts the "sizzle in the sale" and keeps the buyer up at night wondering if he/she has finally found that business he/she has been looking for.

A CBR is mandatory when the purchase price of the business requires a clear delineation of information to a buyer and it is a catalyst that motivates the buyer to move forward to further investigate the industry and the business.

A good CBR will be very detailed in the information it provides and should include:
- ✓ An executive summary
- ✓ The name and address of the company
- ✓ History of the company
- ✓ Information and analysis of the industry and the markets the business operates in
- ✓ Information on the products and services the business provides
- ✓ Details about the distribution channels the business uses
- ✓ Details about the customers the business services
- ✓ Information about the competition
- ✓ Details about the management team that runs the business including any key employees and why they are key
- ✓ Details of any real estate that is part of the business being sold
- ✓ Summary of the profit and loss statements with supporting comments
- ✓ Potential business growth strategies
- ✓ Competitive analysis
- ✓ Conclusion/summary
- ✓ Exhibits or supporting documents to the CBR
- ✓ Photographs

Executive Summary and CBR

An Executive Summary is essentially an "elevator speech" about the business so a buyer can determine if they wish to further their inquiry. If the buyer requires more detailed and sensitive information about the business, the next step is to provide the Confidential Business Review (CBR). Make sure a signed Confidentiality Agreement is in place before providing either an Executive Summary or CBR.

End Of Chapter Notes

Use this page to write down notes, ideas and other brainstorming for selling your business.

Section Five

Finding a Buyer

"Quality questions create a quality life. Successful people ask better questions and as a result they get better answers."

Anthony Robbins, American Author, Peak Performance Expert/Consultant

Introduction

With the planning completed, it is now time to move into the "doing" phase. The steps and approach you take will depend on how quickly you want to make a sale as well as who you want to notify that the business is for sale and how you will get the word out. This is the most difficult part of selling a business as once the market knows the business is for sale, customers, employees, suppliers, creditors, landlords, franchisors (if the business is part of a franchise) and competitors can affect the business and the direction it is going.

Activate Buyer Search Plan

It sounds simplistic, and it is, but you have one business to sell so you only need one buyer. However, according to the California Association of Business Brokers (CABB), it takes approximately 6.6 months to sell a business—if it sells. Plus, only one in every 5.5 businesses listed for sale actually sells. In my experience, it will take at least ten buyer inquiries before you get an offer. If you haven't received an offer after ten buyer inquiries, it probably means something needs to be adjusted with the selling of the business - and generally this is the price as the seller is asking too much.

Each buyer that inquires about buying the business will take a different approach. The goal is to logically address the market to find as many qualified buyers as possible. Places to do this will vary depending on what meets your needs as the seller. Options include the following:
- ✓ Ask family and friends if they know an interested and qualified buyer.
- ✓ Ask your accountant and attorney to see if they know anyone. (Note: Your accountant and attorney may be under codes of ethics and possible legal disclosure constraints so discuss this with them first.)
- ✓ Inquire with groups that you belong such as Rotary, Kiwanis, Apex, Jaycees, etc.
- ✓ Inquire with local chambers of commerce.
- ✓ Inquire with your franchisor (if your business is part of a franchise).
- ✓ Inquire with local business brokers.
- ✓ Place or view ads in national or state trade magazines.
- ✓ Inquire with your national trade association or its local chapter.
- ✓ Place or view ads in special interest magazines such as Inc. Magazine, Entrepreneur or Fortune.
- ✓ Search the World Wide Web.
- ✓ Place or view ads in the "Business Opportunities" section of your local newspapers -though the success of this avenue has greatly diminished due to the World Wide Web.
- ✓ Place or view ads in your local business newspaper or similar business publication.

An interesting option to consider is talking with a competitor. If you choose to explore this option, hire a professional to assist. I learned this lesson the hard way from selling my first business many years ago. A business owner in the same industry showed interest in buying the business. After disclosing all the details about my business, he decided to open a competing location directly across the street. He lasted about 18 months before closing his doors, but not before he frightened away a buyer for my business who was in the process of making an offer. The buyer changed his mind after finding out another competitor was moving into town.

If you hire a professional to assist you with selling your business, make sure you refer any leads to your advisor so he/she can follow through with the appropriate action.

As you receive inquiries from buyers, record their details in the chart below. If a buyer refuses to give you their contact information, don't take the inquiry any further. Imagine how difficult they will be to work with once you get further into the transaction and have to negotiate price and terms or conditions.

Buyer Inquiry Tracker

No.	Inquiry Date	Name	Address	Phone Number	Comment
1					
2					
3					
4					
5					
6					
7					
8					
9					
10					
11					

Distribute The Executive Summary

As you start receiving buyer inquiries, the juggling act begins. Often times the buyer wants as much information as possible without providing too many details, while the seller wants to know all about the buyer before providing any details.

The solution to this problem is to provide the buyer with the Executive Summary. Before you hand over your Executive Summary, you could ask the buyer to answer some general questions just to get a feel for who they are and if they are genuine. It is not unusual to get buyers inquiring about any business for sale even though they have little capacity to strike a deal.

Use the chart below to list questions you would like to ask a potential buyer before you distribute your Executive Summary. Add your own questions if you have items that are important to you. You may want a buyer to complete a Confidentiality Agreement or Non-Disclosure Agreement before you provide the Executive Summary.

Questions	Answers
Have you owned a business before?	
What industries have you worked in?	
What is your management experience?	
How many employees have you managed before?	
How much do you have for a down payment?	
How many businesses have you looked at so far?	

Qualify The Buyer

The buyer made their initial inquiry, received the Executive Summary and now wants more information. A difficult step in the transaction occurs when a seller tries to qualify a buyer. The seller doesn't wish to disclose any more information than necessary in case the buyer is a competitor or is someone who cannot be trusted. Conversely, the buyer doesn't want to disclose too much in case the seller will tell them more and thereby give reasons to lower the offer.

This is also a good reason to have a professional business broker handle the transaction for you. A business broker understands what questions to ask and more importantly, can assess the motivation of the buyer, their ability to do a deal, the type of questions the buyer is asking and the appropriate next steps.

Incidentally, it was common practice prior to the World Wide Web that the buyer would go to the business broker's office for a personal introduction and to review the transaction. E-mail is now the main means of communicating and face-to-face meetings are less common.

The chart below has some suggested questions to qualify a buyer. Add additional questions that you would like to ask.

Questions	Answers
What is your time frame to buy a business?	
Why are you looking to buy at this time?	
Are you looking at just this business or others?	
How much money have you put aside to invest in a business?	
Do you want to be in business for yourself and why?	
Are you currently working?	
Are you making all the decisions or are there others?	

Confidentiality/Non-Disclosure Agreement

Once you have qualified the buyer and decide you are willing to provide more information, it is critical to have the buyer sign a Confidentiality Agreement (also called a Non-Disclosure Agreement or NDA).

Here are a few considerations:

1. Make sure this document is typed and ready to go as the buyer could be looking at other businesses and if they think you are not serious or are difficult to deal with, they may move on.
2. There may be a necessity to explain to the buyer the purpose of the document. If this is the first business they have inquired about, they may not know what it is or its purpose.
3. To get the Confidentiality Agreement to the buyer to read, sign and return to you, send it via fax or e-mail. Sending through the mail is an option but delays the process and allows the buyer to get distracted by other opportunities.
4. While you are collecting the fax number or e-mail address of the buyer, ask additional questions so you can be certain this is a serious buyer.
5. Avoid the temptation to give away information under the assumption that the buyer is going to sign and return the Confidentiality Agreement.
6. Make sure the Confidentiality Agreement is signed and fully completed. Again, this indicates how serious the buyer really is and reflects their attitude.
7. If information is left blank, for whatever reason, it suggests the buyer is not as serious. Be careful about giving out too much information.

---

8 Traits of Serious Buyers

1. They are motivated to buy a business at this time.
2. They know why they want to buy a business.
3. They know specifically what they are looking for and why.
4. They have a specific amount of capital set aside that they are ready to invest.
5. They want to be in business for themselves.
6. They are either unemployed or their job is currently not working for them.
7. They are the decision maker.
8. If financing is required, they have the necessary credit score and creditworthiness to get loan approval.

Determine Buyer Interest

Knowing when and how to contact a buyer to see if he/she is still interested in pursuing the inquiry to buy the business can be challenging. If the seller calls, the buyer thinks the seller is desperate to sell and will therefore accept a lower offer. The buyer may also ask additional questions about the business and use this as leverage in negotiations.

Buying a business is emotional and stressful and puts both the seller and buyer out of their comfort zones. This is one of the top three reasons business owners choose to hire a business broker to help them with the transaction. A good business broker understands the complexity of the transaction and has the knowledge and skill to navigate through the process. A broker is also able to remain emotionally detached and can therefore offer good counsel on decisions to be made.

Use the following chart to track the buyers that followed up on their initial inquiry.

Buyer Inquiry Tracker

No.	1st Inquiry Date	2nd Inquiry Date	Name	Phone Number	Comment
1					
2					
3					
4					
5					
6					
7					
8					
9					
10					
11					
12					

Present Confidential Business Review

Not all businesses require a Confidential Business Review (CBR). The larger the transaction, the more sophisticated the buyer and his support team will be.

If the buyer meets the following criteria, you are ready to provide him with your Confidential Business Review:

✓ The buyer continues to show interest and is asking good questions
✓ The buyer has signed a Confidentiality Agreement
✓ The buyer has been qualified and has demonstrated his/her ability to purchase or put down a deposit to finance the transaction
✓ You are feeling comfortable with the direction everything is going

The easy choice is to mail or fax your CBR to the buyer, but the best option is to schedule a face-to-face meeting with the buyer. This meeting will allow you to talk more about the business and make sure you feel this buyer is genuine. You will also have the opportunity to see the buyer's reaction to the CBR and answer any specific questions.

A qualified and motivated buyer will make the time for an in-person meeting. If the buyer doesn't have the time to meet, then you don't have the time to make the CBR available. It is as simple as that. The CBR contains too much sensitive information that your competitors would love to know and it is not worth the risk.

Final Thought

It would be reasonable to argue that the steps outlined in this section could take place in a different order. The important point is to make sure all of these steps are completed. Any attempts to move into the next phase (making a deal) will fail if these steps are not completed.

End Of Chapter Notes

Use this page to write down notes, ideas and other brainstorming for selling your business.

Forming a Deal

"You name the price and I'll name the terms."

Tom West, American Business Broker Icon

Introduction

Once a buyer has interest in your business and you complete the steps in the previous section, it's time to move the transaction forward. If you're lucky, you may have buyer interest from more than one potential buyer. If this is the case, proceed with caution as some buyers may quickly disappear as they do not wish to be in a competitive situation when making such an important decision. It's not uncommon for the situation to turn quickly and then you will be "back to the drawing board" and seeking new potential buyers.

Buyer Visit And First Meeting

It is quite possible that the buyer has done a "mystery shop" of your business prior to requesting a tour behind the scenes. Before you open your doors and start exposing the underbelly of the business, give some thought to the next steps and make sure you prepare.

First Impressions are Critical

The buyer will have three critical first impressions when meeting you and your business for the first time. The first impression is of the business itself and the buyer's five-second reaction to it. Many conscious and subconscious thought processes happen for the buyer while assessing the following:
- ✓ Location
- ✓ Customers
- ✓ Employees
- ✓ Layout of the store (if applicable)
- ✓ Ambience/ overall feel including the neighboring businesses, sounds/music, smells, etc.

At the same time, the buyer may be considering things to change that they think may make the business better including:
- ✓ Moving around the displays or better positioning of the existing inventory
- ✓ Changing the inventory by bringing in new product lines or eliminating some products

Second Impressions are Just as Critical

The second critical impression for the buyer is the owner of the business. Like it or not, the buyer will be wondering if he/she can manage this business as well or better than you.

During the third and final critical impression, the buyer determines if he/she feels that the answers you are giving to questions are honest and truthful. The buyer wants to ensure that if he/she continues pursuing the possibility of buying the business, you will provide honest and straightforward information.

Tour Of The Business

Before scheduling a tour of your business with a buyer, it is important to prepare. This is your chance to showcase your business and excite the buyer about the industry and business opportunity. You should also use this time to ask questions and make some of your own decisions. These could include:
1. Am I willing to offer selling financing to this buyer?
2. Am I comfortable disclosing some of the more confidential information about the business or is this buyer just wasting my time?
3. Do I trust this person?
4. Is this buyer capable of running my business?

I suggest that as you tour your business with the buyer, you treat him/her like a customer. You want to give a positive perception of the business and also share management information so he/she understands the issues that go with operating this type of business. Plus, you don't want a potential buyer walking out of the business and making negative comments. Also, consider preparing a packet of sales and marketing information—the kind of information that you give your best customers—so the buyer has something tangible to take with them and review later.

Use the following table to have an instant checklist of items you would like to show the buyer to create a positive first impression. Be sure to add your own ideas as it relates to your business. The list could include "must show" items along with a secondary list of things to say if you think the buyer is a good match for your business.

NOTE: Be prepared to wrap up the meeting early if you are not comfortable with the direction it is going.

Business appearance	Sales and marketing material	Information packet
Items unique to your business	Competitive advantages	New ideas you haven't had time to put into operation

And remember, be prepared for your first buyer visit and meeting by:
1. Being professional
2. Being organized
3. Being prepared

Establish Buyer Interest

As the tour of the business comes to a close, try to finish the meeting in a quiet and private place so you can review details of the tour with the buyer and answer any final questions. Keep in mind that the buyer's head is probably spinning from all of the details.

Keys to a Successful Tour

- ✓ Finish the meeting on a positive note.
- ✓ State that the buyer may call to ask follow-up questions, who they may contact, the means of contacting that person and the appropriate time for that contact to be made.
- ✓ The buyer has answers to ALL of their questions.
- ✓ There is agreement on the next steps, who is responsible for each of the steps and by when. This helps each party know what's happening, even if it is just an agreement that the buyer will contact you or your business broker if there is interest in taking their inquiry further.

Five Key Questions to Ask a Qualified Buyer

1. How much money is available as a down payment?
2. Is the money liquid?
3. How soon do you plan on being in business?
4. Who is the decision maker in the purchase?
5. What is your previous management or business ownership experience?

Motivating The Buyer To Act: Offer To Purchase

Question: How do you motivate a buyer to act and make an offer to purchase the business?
Answer: Not very easily.

At this point in the transaction the buyer is responsible for taking the next major step, but there are some strategies you can try:

1. Call and follow up with the buyer to see if there are any questions still outstanding. Each buyer is different so there is no set rule as to how long you need to wait before following up. However, this is where a deal may die as the buyer has little to no reason to take all the risk unless it is something he/she really wants to do—try and understand the buyer's position.
2. If you have an agent working for you, you should expect them to be following up—if it is appropriate. Some buyers like to work through details in their own time and that must be respected. Failure to respect the buyer's request could kill any chances of moving forward.
3. Understand the reasons why the buyer is thinking about buying the business and then make suggestions that benefit both parties. For example, if you want to retire, you might offer to continue working part-time in the business. This may suit a younger buyer eager to own the business as he/she would welcome the additional help from the established owner.

List the reasons your buyer wants to purchase the business so you understand their motivation.

Facilitate Negotiations

If the buyer is ready to make an offer, the dynamics of the relationship between the buyer and seller now change as do those of any other parties in the transaction. Casual comments or conversations from previous meetings may now be remembered as key negotiation points by one party. Misunderstandings can gain more importance than they should as both parties try to position themselves to get the best deal from the situation.

There is no question that a broker or agent is helpful at this juncture since their experience and emotional detachment allows all parties to have clear discussions that can then be transferred onto paper for the proper consideration.

Keeping track of negotiation points is critical so that they can be converted into a legal document for review and agreement. Even with the details in writing, there are still many more steps to go through before the deal closes.

Write down negotiation points as they are discussed so they can be converted into a written offer.

List the reasons your buyer wants to purchase your business so you can understand their motivation.

Letter Of Intent, Asset Purchase Agreement Or Stock Offer

From verbal discussions and scratched notes and what each party thought was what was agreed to, to actually putting it in writing and getting it accepted by both parties, coming to mutual agreement is a huge task.

Emotions play a huge role in the decision to sell or buy a business. At this stage, it is likely that the seller starts thinking that the buyer is not offering enough for the business and the buyer thinks he/she is paying too much.

It is what it is.

But remember, as this all plays out, life is happening. Players in the deal get sick, have vacations planned, have family members that have crises to manage, etc. The bottom line: always show good faith in the deal making process and put yourself in the shoes of the other party. If you can do this, your chances of getting agreement on all negotiation points will be greatly improved.

Once all the discussions that form the basis of a deal are done, it is normally up to the buyer or the buyer's agent to convert the discussions to paper and make a formal written offer for the seller to consider.

In section two we discussed a Stock or Asset Purchase Agreement and Letter of Intent. Whichever option is chosen, like everything else in the deal, this in itself can be a negotiation point. There are different tax implications for both seller and buyer with a Stock Sale vs. Asset Sale. If you are using an attorney or agent, they will be able to make suggestions on the best path to follow for your specific situation.

Keep track of the concerns that are keeping you awake at night.

End Of Chapter Notes

Use this page to write down notes, ideas and other brainstorming for selling your business.

Section Seven

Closing the Deal

"It ain't over till it's over."

Yogi Bera

Introduction

If you have come to this stage in the transaction, hopefully you have a signed offer from the buyer that you have also signed and accepted. If this is the case, you are now ready to let the buyer do their due diligence. The primary purpose of due diligence is to allow the buyer and their advisors the opportunity to inspect all the representations made for their accuracy.

In my experience as a business broker and in talking to colleagues, we estimate that 50% of all deals collapse during the due diligence process. The reasons this happens are many and interestingly come from both the seller and the buyer. The reasons may include:
- ✓ The seller is no longer motivated to sell.
- ✓ The seller's price expectations are too high which the buyer determines by seeing what other businesses are for sale in the same industry.
- ✓ The seller is not honest about their business and/or their situation. For example, a new competitor is entering the market, the rent is too high and making the business unviable or the financial statements do not correspond to what the seller says, etc.
- ✓ Lack of due diligence by the seller. After accepting an offer and talking with their accountant, the seller learns the resulting tax obligations are too high and so they no longer wish to sell.
- ✓ The seller is unwilling to provide financing.
- ✓ The buyer gets cold feet.
- ✓ The buyer is unable to get financing.
- ✓ The buyer doesn't believe what the seller is representing.
- ✓ The buyer spoke to a "family expert" or "friend" who said that it wasn't a good idea to buy a business.

There is no hard and fast rule, but the due diligence period should take anywhere from one to three weeks, with about two weeks being the norm. Be patient; it is also not uncommon for a buyer to use due diligence as an opportunity to revisit every question previously asked.

There is even the request from some buyers to "test drive" the business to see if they like it. This should not be allowed to happen for many reasons. For example, if there are employees in the business, they can become unsettled. When regular customers see a new person in the business, it leads to obvious questions. If the buyer was injured while on site, it would create a worker's compensation problem. And so the reasons go on.

Role of the Parties

If the seller has been using a business broker to assist with the sale, it is important that they be the conduit between both parties. It is the buyer's right to ask for any information that relates to the operation of the business and to ask questions about the financial information. Buyers should bring their own professional, such as an accountant, to review the books. It is not the role of the business broker to provide that service.

Open Due Diligence

Opening due diligence happens once both the seller and buyer have reached written agreement on the price and terms of the sale of the business. An agreement can be verbal but I would discourage either party from moving forward with Due Diligence until a written and signed purchase agreement has been signed by both parties. It's interesting to me that when each party verbally agrees on a certain set of criteria, that when that apparently same agreement is put into words there no longer is an agreement.

The purpose of Due Diligence is that it allows both parties to inspect documents that hopefully reflect and support all the verbal discussions between both parties leading up to the signing of the purchase agreement. I would also add that the Due Diligence goes both ways. If the buyer has made claims that the owner has relied upon to sign the purchase agreement and finds the buyer made false claims they can cancel the agreement or re-negotiate the terms. Generally, however, the buyer is using Due Diligence to verify the claims of the seller and work out their next steps with some of the terms of the purchase agreement. These next steps could involve talking with the landlord about the lease, working with the lender to continue the loan approval process, working with the franchisor if a franchisee is involve and so on.

A good agreement should detail what the buyer wants to see as well as what the seller wants. It should also require the buyer to provide proof that he/she has a cash down payment to open escrow once Due Diligence is complete plus a copy of the buyer's credit score and personal disclosure if the offer is subject to the buyer obtaining a loan or the seller is being asked to carry a note.

A comprehensive checklist is provided over the next three pages. The list is extensive so not all items will apply to your situation. You may need to add your own items as they relate to your transaction, but the checklist should give you a great start. Also, be sure to make a list of any items you would like the buyer to disclose to you.

Write down questions you have about the due diligence process.

Due Diligence Checklist

Organizational Matters

1. Articles of Incorporation amendments/restatements
2. Bylaws/amendments
3. Current domestic stock statement or equivalent
4. Stock transfers ledger
5. Buy-Sell agreements/shareholder agreements
6. Stock restriction agreements
7. Voting Trusts
8. Oral understandings regarding any of the above

Title/Lease Asset Documents

9. Real property deeds
10. List/description of real properties owned
11. Real property leases
12. List/description of real properties occupied
13. List/description of general assets (by type)
14. Bills of Sale/or invoices for equipment and/or inventory stock in trade
15. Automobile and truck registrations
16. List/description of automobiles and trucks owned
17. Automobile and truck leases
18. List/description of automobile and trucks leased
19. Other vehicle/vessels/rolling equipment or machinery leases
20. List/description of other vehicle/vessels/rolling equipment or machinery
21. Office equipment leases (telephone, copy machines, etc.)
22. List/description of office equipment leased

23. Industrial equipment leases
24. List/description of industrial equipment leased
25. Furniture leases
26. List/description of furniture
27. Patent/trademark/service mark registrations
28. List/description of patents, trademarks and service marks
29. Bill of Landing for inventory stock in trade
30. List/description of inventory/stock in trade (type, item and location)
31. List/description of raw materials on hand
32. List/description of raw materials on order
33. Other leases or use agreements not mentioned above
34. List/description of all other assets not mentioned above

Encumbrances

35. Trust deeds
36. Security agreements
37. UCC-1 finance statements
38. Stock pledge agreements
39. Loan documents (including applications)
40. Notes made or held by the company
41. Line of credit agreements
42. Guarantees (company and personal)
43. Notices of default
44. Oral understandings regarding any of the foregoing

Licenses/Permits

45. City business licenses/permits
46. City industrial/occupational permits
47. State industrial/occupational permits
48. State licenses/permits

49. Federal licenses/permits (FCC, etc).
50. Correspondences to/from any state or federal body governing the business or operations of the company.

Business Contracts

51. License agreements.
52. Royalty agreements.
53. Patent/trademark/service mark assignments.
54. Dealership agreements.
55. Distributorship agreements.
56. Vendor agreements.
57. Supplier agreements.
58. Consulting agreements.
59. Employment agreements.
60. Independent contractor agreements.
61. Asset sale/purchase agreements.
62. Employee stock sale/purchase agreements.
63. Employee stock subscription agreements.
64. Employee stock option plans.
65. Employee stock option agreements.
66. Pension/profit sharing trust or agreements.
67. Medical/reimbursement plans, agreements.
68. Trust indentures.
69. Oral understandings regarding any of the foregoing.

Litigation/Adverse Claims

70. Plaintiff suits – pleadings, discovery, etc.
71. Defendant suits – pleadings, discovery, etc.
72. Attorney audit response letters.
73. Demand letters received/sent.
74. Labor board proceeding documents.

75. Administrative court proceeding documents.
76. Notices of default received.
77. Foreclosure/private sale documents.
78. Collection letters/dunning letters utilized (form or otherwise).
79. Collection letters/dunning letters received.
80. Bankruptcy filing documents.

Financial/Tax

81. Three (3) years prior state tax returns.
82. Three (3) years prior Federal tax returns.
83. Franchise tax board suspension review documents.
84. Real property tax assessment notices/documents.
85. Personal property/business equipment tax assessment notices/documents.
86. Three (3) years prior financial statements.
87. Interim financial statements.
88. Tax delinquency notices.
89. Audit inquiry response letters.
90. Summary of all deposit accounts, savings accounts and other accounts.
91. Six (6) month prior bank statements (all accounts).
92. Daily check registers/account books (including computer stored information).
93. General ledger books (including computer stored information).
94. Special account ledge books.
95. Chart of accounts.
96. Daily/weekly chronological financial records.
97. Copy of credit reference materials provided by vendors, etc.
98. List of company credit cards and holders.

99. List of vendors supplying company on account (with balances and A/R aging)
100. Ledgers showing company A/R with aging
101. Ledgers showing company A/P with aging

Securities

102. State securities permits/notices/filings
103. State securities registrations/ qualifications
104. Federal securities registration/offering circulars/disclosure documents
105. Federal securities compliance documents (10K, 10Q, etc.)
106. Correspondence to/from the New York department of corporations
107. Correspondence to/from the SEC
108. Correspondence to/from any foreign body governing securities matters

General

109. Attorney retainer letters/ correspondence
110. Attorney opinion letter prepared with regard to the company
111. Accountant retainer letter/ correspondence
112. Accountant "working papers" pertaining to previous three (3) years financial statements
113. Insurance policies including business liabilities, disability, medical and workers compensation policies
114. Detail of key management employees: names, addresses, ages, work experience, positions held, job description, salary and benefits

115. General information regarding employees: number of employees (full-time and part-time) by each location and department, percentage of employees who have left company and reasons for departure, working hours and wage levels by position and department
116. Past history of labor problems
117. Details of employees benefits (pensions, bonuses, retirement plans, etc.)
118. Policy manuals or materials
119. Company operational or procedure manuals or materials
120. Employee manuals or materials
121. Employment applications and hiring forms, documents or materials
122. Employment disclosure documents
123. Past and present business plans for company
124. Full organizational chart of company
125. Details of internal operational structures including identity of who plans, checks and carries out functions, who reviews their results, and how the foregoing is accomplished:
a. Management structure
b. Marketing structure
c. Purchasing structure
d. Merchandising structure
126. Particular details of marketing/sales structures, methods and programs, including identity and functions of sales personnel, special or unusual promotional activities, occasional programs and other special sales efforts
127. Materials or substantial contracts of agreements (written or oral) not listed above or otherwise disclosed

Secure Finance…If Necessary

With all the items on the checklist to take care of, often a key component of the deal is the buyer securing financing.

For the lender to accept a request from the buyer to apply for a loan, the buyer will need:
- ✓ An application form from the lender that the buyer needs to complete
- ✓ Proof of the required down payment in cash (and possible supporting document to show where the deposit comes from such as savings or a gift from a family member.)
- ✓ A minimum credit score acceptable to the lender
- ✓ Buyer supporting documents for the loan such as tax returns, payroll stubs to show previous wages and income, business plan, confirmation that the landlord is prepared to assign the lease to the buyer, plus other documents the lender will detail as it relates to the specific transaction.

Securing a loan can be a delaying and detailed process. If the business has been pre-qualified for a loan, then using a football analogy, you have moved to the seller's 20 yard line. If the buyer completes the application and receives a pre-qualification letter from the bank, both parties move to the 50 yard line.

The next step is to get a pre-approval letter that says the lender likes the business and likes the buyer for the business, moving the action to the buyer's 20 yard line. The next play is to complete due diligence, get lender instructions and get to the 10 yard line. Now the final play is to open escrow, dot the I's and T's and run the ball into the end zone for a touchdown by completing the transaction—with everyone celebrating.

> **Write down questions about the financing process so you can check later.**

Obtain Lender Instructions

As we just mentioned, when third party financing is involved, the lender will require a lot of documents. While most of these are provided by the buyer, the seller is also required to provide some documentation. As the process continues, the lender may request even more documents and more information. As the owner of the business, be patient with the process and supply all documents as quickly and readily as you can so the process keeps moving.

Just so you know, if a third party lender provides financing, the time to process all the paperwork and get approval can take anywhere from 30 to 60 days, with 45 days being about the norm. If the third party lender is a loan from the Small Business Administration, there are strict processes for the lender to follow with no shortcuts allowed. Bottom line: Respond as quickly and professionally as you can, otherwise you may end up killing the transaction.

Track requests you receive for seller documents:

Open Escrow

The escrow process is not the same in all fifty US States. In some states an attorney provides the escrow service and may be known as a "transaction attorney." In some states, like California, there are companies that specialize in offering escrow services just like the escrow service when you buy and sell a residential property, but their focus is on commercial transactions.

What does the escrow company do?

1. Serves as a neutral party in the transaction. Their role includes a communication link between all parties in the transaction including seller, buyer, franchisor, landlord, business broker, lending institution, etc.
2. Prepares escrow instructions and amendments.
3. Requests publication, recording and UCC lien searches.
4. Complies with third party lender requirements.
5. Requests a beneficiary statement if the buyer is taking over a debt or other obligation.
6. Receives purchase funds from the buyer and holds them in trust.
7. Pro-rates taxes, interest, rents and reimburses the seller for their lease security deposit.
8. Secures release of all contingencies or other conditions that are part of the transaction.
9. Closes escrow when all instructions of the buyer and seller have been executed including:
    a. Bill of Sale
    b. Assignment of Lease, sub-lease or new lease
    c. Abandonment of Fictitious Business Name
    d. Clearances from State Board of Equalization, Employment Development Department and Franchise Tax Board (or the equivalent in each state).
10. Disburses funds as authorized by instructions and prepares a statement showing how funds were dispersed.
11. Records UCC-1 and UCC-3, if necessary.

If you have questions about the escrow process, write them down to research further:

Start Bulk Sale Process

If the business is being sold under an Asset Purchase Agreement or all the assets of the business are being purchased by the buyer, then the escrow company may want to execute the Bulk Sale requirements. If the business is being sold as a Stock Sale, this is not required.

Business transactions are considered personal property and are governed under the Uniform Commercial Code (or UCC) that came into effect to synchronize commercial transactions within the 50 States. This was deemed a legal necessity from earlier times as more and more business was done outside each state. For example, a company could buy a product from a company in state A for to use in a manufacturing plant in state B. The final product is then warehoused in state C but sold from state D for final delivery to state E. Once again, different states have different processes and different names for it, but the purpose is to prevent any funds from being transferred to the seller until the provisions of the state Bulk Sale process have been met.

The bottom line is that the deal can't close until the Bulk Sale requirements are met. Depending on holidays and the lead time required to meet publication deadlines, it will take a minimum of twelve business days which typically equates to about a 21 day period.

At the time of starting the Bulk Sale process, the escrow company will deal with getting state agency releases from states that collect state taxes, employment or wage taxes, state income taxes, local county taxes, etc. They will also perform searches to make sure there are no loans, leases, liens or judgments that affect the personal property or assets of the business being transferred to the buyer.

If you have questions about the Bulk Sale process, write them down here:

Purchase Price Allocation

One item that needs to be addressed prior to closing escrow is the Purchase Price Allocation. This is a statement from both the seller and the buyer describing how the total purchase price will be broken down for tax reporting purposes. There may also be other implications. For example, in California, sales tax needs to be paid on the fixtures, furniture and equipment. If the current rate is 7.75% and the value of the FF&E is agreed at $100,000, the buyer will need to pay $7,750.00 in sales tax—a hidden cost most buyers don't anticipate when starting their journey to buy a business.

Can agreeing with the buyer on how to allocate the purchase price kill the deal? Absolutely! However, we are now in escrow and need to make that final allocation. Hopefully it has been discussed by the seller and the buyer prior to this point so both parties are in agreement, but it is decision time so it needs to be dealt with now.

Write down the Purchase Price Allocation if this is yet to be done.

Sign Final Documents

If the stars are aligned with the planets and the moon, it is now necessary to meet at the escrow company requirements so all the legal documents can be executed and the payment and transfer of money takes place. Normally this is done on the day prior to ownership transferring from the seller to the buyer, but there can be reasons why this is varied. For example, if the lender wants a signed copy of all documents before they will release funds to the escrow company, the timeline can be affected.

Once the escrow company receives final payment from the buyer and lender, they will then have the responsibility of transferring and paying any taxes, transfer fees and business broker commissions. They will also make adjustments for the number of days to be refunded to the seller because the change of possession takes place prior to the start of a new month, etc.

The escrow company, on the day of signing documents, will provide an itemized account of all monies received and to be paid so both the seller and buyer can make sure it is all in order.
And here's the good news: if you get through this day with all documents being signed, confirmation that the lender is transferring funds and all other conceivable items have been addressed, then congratulations are in order—you have sold your business!

Don't underestimate those final nerves—from all parties. It is not unheard of for a buyer not to come to the escrow company to sign the final documents simply because they cannot go through with the transaction.

Write down any questions you have about the final document signing process:

End Of Chapter Notes

Use this page to write down notes, ideas and other brainstorming for selling your business.

Section Eight

Final Steps

"*The critical ingredient is to get off your butt and do something. It's as simple as that. A lot of people have ideas, but there are few who decide to do something about them now. Not tomorrow. Not next week. But today. The true Entrepreneur is a doer, not a dreamer.*"

Nolan Bushnell, American Businessman, Founder of Atari Computer

Introduction

If all the legal documents are signed by all parties in the transaction, the buyer has deposited their funds with the escrow company and the lender has funded a loan (if applicable), then the business is ready for Change of Possession from the seller to the buyer. And the seller can get their proceeds from the sale, right?

Not just yet.

Seller Proceeds From The Sale

The seller may have a few items to finalize before the escrow company can pay the proceeds from the sale. For the state of California, these include:

1. Certificate of Payment of Sales and Use Tax from the State Board of Equalization
2. Certificate of Release from the Employment Development Department
3. Certificate of Release from the Franchise Tax Board for Corporations and LLCs

Different escrow companies have different ways of handling the above. Check with yours a few days prior to escrow closing so you know what's expected of you and you can plan to get it done. Some escrow companies may hold all the seller proceeds until all items are up to date while others may hold a sizeable amount as incentive for the seller to get these items addressed.

Final Checklist

On the following page is the beginning of a checklist. This is for items that will probably require some attention after the business changes possession. The checklist is not exhaustive but gives a good starting point with room for you to add other items as they relate to the business you've just sold.

And by the way, congratulations! If you are reading this part of the guide because your transaction has come to this point, then your business is now sold.

Well done!

Final Checklist

Once the seller receives the proceeds from the sale, the biggest remaining item is most likely the delivery of any training that the buyer negotiated as part of the deal. However, it is also time to make sure all the remaining tasks in the business are addressed.

The following checklist captures some of the tasks. Make sure you add tasks that apply to your business so you can close them down. Use the chart below to record who you spoke to and when.

Description	Start Date	Completion Date	Contact
Redirect personal mail			
Remove personal e-mail address from any business e-mail software			
Update cell phone numbers—if transferring with the sale to the buyer			
Check if voicemail messages need changing			
Notify gas company for final meter read			
Notify telephone company (local)			
Notify telephone company (long distance)			
Notify credit card provider (if applies)			
Notify suppliers (if applies)			
Cancel any lines of credit (if applies)			
Cancel any business insurance policies			
Cancel any advertising not required as part of the sale			

End Of Chapter Notes

Use this page to write down notes, ideas and other brainstorming for selling your business.

Financial Statements: Recasting Exercise

> *"In order to succeed, your desire for success should be greater than your fear of failure."*
>
> *Bill Cosby, Comedian and Activist*

Introduction

This section is included for the curious. The explanation and information provided may be considered technical and has been added to provide a reasonable explanation of the term Discretionary Earnings. If you are not interested, read no further.

For a profitable business to sell, it must have an asking or list price. For those that trade on the stock market and are used to prices of stocks, you will be familiar with EBIT and EBITDA terminology. However, when selling a business, the starting point for a valuation is the amount of Discretionary Earnings (DE). This is the methodology used by the International Business Brokers Association and the various affiliated state associations including the California Association of Business Brokers.

Discretionary Earnings are defined as:
- ✓ Net Income Before Taxes,
- ✓ Depreciation and Amortization,
- ✓ Interest,
- ✓ Owner's (one owner) Compensation, and
- ✓ IRS Code Section 179 (non-recurring expenses).

From a business valuation perspective, the difference between Discretionary Earnings (DE) and EBITDA is that for public companies it includes the management expense at fair market value, whereas for private companies it includes owner's compensation and perks.

DE does not equal EBITDA—they are completely different and should not be confused. You arrive at DE by recasting the financial statements, that is, Income Statement and/or tax returns and the Balance Sheet. Recasting means taking the numbers from these financial statements and using only the true income and costs needed to run the business.

But why do we need to know the amount of the business Discretionary Earnings?
1. Discretionary Earnings "normalizes" the income the business produces to provide a more accurate picture of the cash available to a buyer and the real value of the assets.
2. Business owners want to minimize their taxes; therefore they claim as many expenses as possible to reduce their taxable income.
3. It provides protection for the buyer. For example, the owner may own the property that is not being sold with the business but has not been expensing an amount for rent. The seller charges $2,000 per month for the lease so this has to be "normalized" into the Discretionary Earnings. Another example is the seller may be using a spouse or friend to "help" in the business but not pay them anything. A buyer needs to replace that free labor at a cost which should be part of the "normal" operating cost of the business.
4. Recasting helps buyers compare "apples with apples."

Instructions

The Discretionary Earnings is the basis for the financial strength and selling price of your business. When buying a privately held company, the buyer will use this number to determine the financial attractiveness of your business when compared to other businesses that are for sale. The buyer will also use this information during due diligence to compare the numbers against the tax return and other financial statements.

On the following page is a blank worksheet and following that, a sample worksheet has been provided for your reference. If you have your tax returns and Profit and Loss statement you can calculate your own Discretionary Earnings.

Here are the steps to follow:
1. Round all numbers to the nearest dollar.
2. Label the headings with the year or period that the column applies. For example, in YTD Current Year add "2008." In the next column show "2007," in the next "2006," or whatever is appropriate.
3. Review lines 5 through 8 and write in these numbers as shown on the tax return.
4. Review lines 11 through 23 and again write in these numbers from the tax return. Add backs are items that the owner or seller has paid through the business but are not true business expenses. They are paid through the business because the business has the cash flow to support it and/or it reduces the owner's taxable income. They lower the value of the business, hence the reason they are added back. The seller must be able to prove these items to the buyer's satisfaction. Add backs are also onetime expenses that reflect unusual or non-recurring expenses a new owner will not be required to pay.
5. Review lines 25 & 26 in case there are adjustments in the favor of the buyer that you need to include.
6. Add together lines 5, 6, 7 & 8 to arrive at a total at Line 9.
7. Now add line 4 plus line 9 plus any amounts shown from line 11 through 23 and deduct any amounts shown at lines 25 & 26 to get a total of Discretionary Earnings.

Remember, Discretionary Earnings are defined as:
- ✓ Net Income Before Taxes,
- ✓ Depreciation and Amortization,
- ✓ Interest,
- ✓ Owner's (one owner) Compensation, and
- ✓ IRS Code Section 179 (non-recurring expenses).

		YTD Current Year	20..	20..	20..
1	Sales				
2	Less Cost of Sales or Cost of Goods				
3	Less Total Operating Expenses				
4	**= Net Income or Pretax Profit**				
5	Plus Depreciation				
6	Plus Amortization				
7	Plus Interest				
8	Plus Owners Salary or Draw				
9	**= Adjusted Earnings**				
10	**Add back** the following **(if applicable)**				
11	Plus Payroll Tax Paid on Owners Salary				
12	Plus Benefits Paid to Owner (i.e. Health Ins)				
13	Auto—Owners Personal Expenses				
14	Auto—Owners Insurance				
15	Auto repairs—Owners Personal Expense				
16	Charitable Contributions				
17	Rent—Adjust to Fair Market Rate				
18	Insurance—Owners Personal Health, Life, etc.				
19	Retirement Plans—Owner Paid Contributions				
20	Plus Meals and Entertainment				
21	Plus Travel—non-related business				
22	Plus Telephone and Cell Phone—non business				
23	Plus one time charges (i.e. bad debt, etc.)				
24					
25	**Less the following (If applicable)**				
26	Market Rate for Non-paid Family or Friends				
27	Market Rent if Rent Charged is Below Market				
28					
29					
30	**Total Discretionary Earnings**				

Example

		YTD Current Year	2007	2006	2005
1	Sales		565,000	550000	500,000
2	Less Cost of Sales or Cost of Goods		170,000	165,000	150,000
3	Less Total Operating Expenses		335,000	330,000	300,000
4	**= Net Income or Pretax Profit**		60,000	55,000	50,000
5	Plus Depreciation		20,000	20,000	20,000
6	Plus Amortization		5,000	5,000	5,000
7	Plus Interest		5,000	5,000	5,000
8	Plus Owners Salary or Draw		80,000	77,000	75,000
9	**= Adjusted Earnings**		170,000	162,000	155,000
10	**Add back** the following **(if applicable)**				
11	Plus Payroll Tax Paid on Owners Salary		8,000	7,700	7,500
12	Plus Benefits Paid to Owner (i.e. Health Ins)		2,500	2,000	2,000
13	Auto—Owners Personal Expenses		3,500	3,300	3,000
14	Auto—Owners Insurance		2,200	2,000	2,000
15	Auto repairs—Owners Personal Expense				
16	Charitable Contributions		800	650	500
17	Rent—Adjust to Fair Market Rate				
18	Insurance—Owners Personal Health, Life, etc.		1,200	1,000	1,000
19	Retirement Plans—Owner Paid Contributions		5,500	5,000	5,000
20	Plus Meals and Entertainment		1,500	1,400	1,400
21	Plus Travel—non-related business		3,500	3,000	3,000
22	Plus Telephone and Cell Phone—non business				
23	Plus one time charges (i.e. bad debt, etc.)				
24					
25	**Less** the following (If applicable)				
26	Market Rate for Non-paid Family or Friends		-8,500	-8,250	-8,000
27	Market Rent if Rent Charged is Below Market				
28					
29					
30	**Total Discretionary Earnings**		190,200	179,800	172,400

End Of Chapter Notes

Use this page to write down notes, ideas and other brainstorming for selling your business.

Section Ten

Additional Information

"*Apply yourself. Get all the education you can get, but then, by God, do something. Don't just stand there, make it happen.*"

Lee Iacocca

Introduction

The following introduces a few different options that may be of interest to a seller when looking for sources of third party finance. The information could also be given to a buyer so they can explore further themselves. Third party finance options are many and varied but here a few highlights.

It is also not unusual for a small business transaction to incorporate a mix of funds. For example, the buyer puts down 15% of the purchase price, the seller carries back 10% and the balance of the purchase price comes from a third party loan from a lender. Like all things in the deal, this is a negotiation.

SBA Programs

The Small Business Administration (SBA) has a range of loan programs available for qualifying businesses. There are two types of lenders: a Non-Preferred Lender and a Preferred Lender. Finding a Preferred Lender is generally the best option as these lenders are empowered to make credit decisions for the SBA. Preferred Lenders include banks, national lenders such as CIT, and popular small business and regional lenders such as Comerica and PNC.

There are extensive rules and regulations to follow that cover the SBA loan program and the lenders are also subject to conflicts of interest and ethical requirements. For example, it is very difficult for a buyer to borrow funds if they have a federal felony conviction. It is also highly unlikely to obtain a loan approval if it is to buy "a house of ill-repute," as it was called in the old days. Sex may sell but it doesn't mean you can get an SBA loan to borrow money to buy a business that engages in it.

To purchase a small business, the loan is usually either a 7(a) or 504 loan. A 7(a) loan is available to purchase a business between $25,000 and $2,000,000. However, a lot of lenders are not interested in loans under $100,000 due to the high cost of processing and meeting compliance requirements. If real estate is involved, a 504 loan would be used and the deal can go up to $6,000,000 in total finance.

For a buyer to be eligible for an SBA loan they must:
- ✓ Intend to run the business (it must be owner operated, not an investment),
- ✓ Be a US citizen (resident aliens may apply but INS gets involved, taking more time),
- ✓ Be at least 21 years old, and
- ✓ The business must have cash flow to meet the debt service.

For more information on the SBA programs, visit: http://www.sba.gov

Other Finance Options

BORSA

BORSA stands for Business Owners Retirement Savings Account. This is a tool which allows you to fund the purchase of a franchise, business start-up or business property using your holdings in your 401(a) pension, profit sharing 401(k), 403(b), 457, IRA rollover or Roth IRA. Through the utilization of a BORSA, these purchases can be accomplished without distributions, taxes, penalties or the use of loans.

A leading provider of BORSA programs is DRDA. You can get more information from their website at http://www.drdacpa.com.

Guidant Financial Group

If the buyer of your business is looking for funds to purchase the business, one option may be to use the existing funds in their IRA. Guidant Financial Group is able to advise a buyer on how to use a self-directed structure to access their retirement funds.

For more information, visit the Guidant website at http://www.guidantfinancial.com.

SD Cooper

The buyer's 401K or IRA account may be used to fund the purchase of a business including starting a new franchise. SD Cooper provides a service that allows a buyer to put the right structure in place. For more information, visit their website at http://www.sdcooper.com.

Sample Documents

I would suggest that it is impossible to successfully do business today without clear and full disclosure. The following two documents could be used if this is important to you and the parties you are dealing with.

Ethics Agreement

The Seller wishes to sell and the Buyer wishes to buy either real property and/or personal property, that is a business, herein called assets. The Seller advises they hold legal title to the assets. To allow each party to see if they wish to enter into an Asset Purchase Agreement or similar instrument, this Ethics Agreement requires that any material fact that could affect a reasonable Buyer's decision to purchase the assets must be disclosed. It is further agreed that each party shall avoid exaggeration, misrepresentation, or concealment of pertinent facts relating to these assets.

Furthermore, this Ethics Agreement may be supplemented by a Confidentiality Agreement (or Non Disclosure Agreement) if this is a request from either party to this agreement.

_____   _____   _____   _____
Seller Signature   Date   Buyer Signature   Date

_____   _____
Seller Name   Buyer Name

_____   _____
Company   Company

_____   _____
Street Address   Street Address

_____   _____
City, State, ZIP   City, State, ZIP

_____   _____
Telephone Number   Telephone Number

Confidentiality Agreement

I, _____ (INSERT NAME), as the undersigned, individually and on behalf of any affiliated prospective Buyer, hereby request information on the following business _____ (INSERT NAME).

Such information shall be provided to the undersigned for the sole purpose of entering into discussions with Seller of said Business for the possible purchase by the undersigned of all or part of the stock or assets of the Business. As used herein, the term Buyer ("Buyer") applies to the undersigned and any partnership, corporation, individual, or other entity which the undersigned is affiliated. The undersigned agrees as follows:

1. NON-DISCLOSURE OF INFORMATION: The undersigned acknowledges that Seller desires to maintain the confidentiality of the information disclosed. ***The undersigned agrees not to disclose or permit access to any Confidential Information without the prior written consent of Seller, to anyone other than Buyer's legal counsel, Accountants, lenders or advisors to whom disclosure or access is necessary for Buyer to evaluate the Business, provided that they are not one of Seller's employees, customers, Landlords, suppliers, or competitors.*** Disclosure of Confidential Information shall be made to these parties only in connection with the potential acquisition of the Business, and then only if these parties understand and agree to maintain the confidentiality of such Confidential Information. The undersigned shall be responsible for any breach of this Agreement by these parties, and neither Buyer nor these parties shall use or permit the use of Confidential Information in any manner whatsoever, except as may be required for Buyer to evaluate the Business or as may be required by legal process. If the Buyer does not purchase the Business, Buyer, at the close of negotiations, will destroy or return to Broker (at Broker's option) all information provided to Buyer and will not retain any copy, reproduction, or record thereof.

2. DEFINITION OF "CONFIDENTIAL INFORMATION": The term "Confidential Information" shall mean all information, including the fact that the Business is for sale, all financial, production, marketing and pricing information, business methods, business manuals, manufacturing procedures, correspondence, processes, data, contracts, customer lists, employee lists and any other information whether written, oral or otherwise made known to Buyer: (a) from any inspection, examination, or other review of the books, records, assets, liabilities, processes, or production methods of Seller; (b) from communications with Seller or its directors, officers, employees, agents, suppliers, customers or representatives; (c) during visits to Seller's premises; or, (d) through disclosure or discovery in any other manner. However, Confidential Information does not include any information which is readily available and known to the public.

3. FURTHER TERMS: ***Neither Buyer nor Buyer's agents will contact Seller's employees, customers, Landlords, competitors or suppliers without Seller's consent.*** For three years, Buyer shall not directly or indirectly solicit for employment any employees of Seller. Seller is specifically intended to be a beneficiary of the duties and obligations of this Agreement and may prosecute any action at law or in equity necessary to enforce its terms and conditions as though a party hereto. Seller may assign this Agreement to any new ownership of the Business. This Agreement can only be modified in writing, signed by both Broker and Buyer. Waiver of any breach of this Agreement shall not be a waiver of any subsequent breach. This Agreement supersedes all prior understandings or agreements between the parties with respect to its subject matter. If Buyer is a corporation, partnership, or other such entity, the undersigned executes this Agreement on behalf of Buyer and warrants that he/she is duly authorized to do so. **Buyer acknowledges receipt of a fully completed copy of this Agreement.**

Buyer Signature	Buyer Name (Please Print) Date
Company	Business Telephone Fax:
Street Address	Home Telephone
City, State, ZIP	Email Address
Buyer Name	

Glossary

The following glossary references some of the terms you may come across as you sell your business.

➤ **Accelerated Depreciation:** Accounting term. It describes a method of depreciation that provides larger deductions from assets in their earlier years of the life compared to the straight-line method.

➤ **Account:** In the bookkeeping sense, account means a basic category of information in which the financial effects of transactions are recorded. For example, consider a checkbook. It provides an account or itemization of the cash inflows and outflows of the balance of your checking account such as health expense, rent expense, entertainment expense, cash, etc.

➤ **Accounting Method:** A process under which income and expenses are determined for tax purposes. This includes both the cash and accrual procedures.

➤ **Accounting Period:** The 12-month period that a taxpayer uses to determine federal income tax liability.

➤ **Accounts Payable (AP):** Amount of money owed to suppliers by the owner of the business that are not paid for by cash but on terms of credit agreed to by both parties.

➤ **Accounts Receivable (AR):** Amount of money owed by customers to the owner of the business that is not paid for by cash but on terms of credit agreed to by both parties.

➤ **Accrual Method of Accounting:** One of the two most common methods of accounting. Under this method, income is reported in the tax year earned, whether or not received, and deductions are claimed in the tax year incurred, whether or not paid.

➤ **Accrued Interest:** Interest that has been earned but not yet paid or credited.

➤ **Adjusted Basis:** The cost or other original basis of property reduced by adjustments—such as depreciation—allowed or allowable and increased by capital improvements and other adjustments.

➤ **Alternative Minimum Tax (AMT):** The tax designed to prevent taxpayers from escaping a fair share of tax liability by use of certain tax breaks. A taxpayer is subject to this tax if they have certain minimum tax adjustments or tax preference items and his/her alternative minimum taxable income exceeds the exemption allowed for his/her filing status and income level.

➤ **Amortization:** Similar to depreciation but applies to intangible assets such as leasehold improvements.

➤ **Asset:** Anything owned that has economic value such as a truck, cash, inventory, etc.

➤ **Assumed Name:** *see DBA*

- **Audited Financial Statements:** Performing detailed tests of financial records and transactions in accordance with generally accepted auditing standards such as GAAP. *Also see Compilation and Review Financial Statements.*

- **Bad Debt:** Business accounts receivable that have been included in income in a prior year that are uncollectible, legally binding debts owed to the taxpayer that are totally worthless and uncollectible.

- **Balance Sheet (BS):** A statement of the financial status of the business on a certain date ("snapshot").

- **Basis:** The amount assigned to an asset from which gain or loss is determined for income tax purposes when the asset is sold. For assets acquired by purchase, this is cost including other allowed adjustments such as depreciation.

- **Blue Sky:** That portion of a "claimed" value or requested price that cannot be supported or generally shown to exist through the application of established valuation methodology. Blue sky is different from Goodwill.

- **Boot:** Cash or property type not included in the definition of a non-taxable exchange.

- **Book Value:** The depreciated value of an asset found on the balance sheet. This can be calculated by subtracting accumulated depreciation from the cost of the related asset.

- **Capital Expenditure:** Expenditure made for assets with useful lives of more than one year. This expenditure may not be deducted in the year it is paid, even if it is paid in connection with a trade or business.

- **Capital Improvement:** An improvement made to an asset to extend the useful life of a property to add to its value. A major repair, such as the replacement of a roof, is an example of such an improvement.

- **Capitalize:** Treating the cost of additions and improvements to property as a capital improvement.

- **Cash Basis Accounting:** A method of accounting wherein income and expenses are recognized, within the statements, when the business receives the income or pays the expense. *Also see Accrual Basis Accounting.*

- **Cash Flow:** Basically, the business' net income plus non-cash charges (depreciation, amortization, and depletion). It can be defined as before or after such items as taxes, debt service (interest only or principal and interest) or extraordinary items. (Should not be confused with Net Cash Flow, a.k.a. Free Cash Flow.)

- **Cash Flow Statement:** A financial statement that displays the sources and use of cash. The Cash Flow Statement groups together cash flows in all activities into three categories: Operations, Financing, and Investments.

- **Cash Method of Accounting:** One of the two most common methods of accounting with the other being Accrual. Under this method of accounting, income is reported in the tax year received and expenses are deducted in the tax year paid.

- **Chart of Accounts:** The formal index of all the accounts used by the business to record its transactions.

- ➤ **Compilation (Financial Statements):** Financial statements and information that is provided by the business owner. *Also see Review and Audit.*

- ➤ **Common Stock:** Shares of ownership in a corporation that entitles holder to residual dividends, after bonds and preferred stock have first received interest and dividends. A stockholder with this type stock usually has a vote in deciding company affairs, including the election of a corporation's board of directors.

- ➤ **Copyright:** Form of protection under the law for authors to protect "original works of authorship." This protection is available for both published and unpublished works.

- ➤ **Constructive Report:** The gauge for a cash-basis taxpayer that determines if income is to be taxed.

- ➤ **Corporation:** A legal business entity owned by shareholders with the ability to own property, incur debts and sue or be sued. For income tax purposes, this term includes associations, trusts that have a majority of corporate characteristics, joint stock companies and insurance companies.

- ➤ **Cost of Goods Sold/Cost of Sales** (CGS, COGS, COS): A grouping of expenses applicable to the materials and labor incorporated directly in the goods or services delivered and sold.

- ➤ **DBA (Doing Business As):** An assumed name under which a business conducts business. For example, Billy Bob Enterprises, Inc. DBA Billy Bob's Hot Dog Grill and Bar.

- ➤ **Depreciation:** The deduction of a reasonable allowance for the wear and tear of assets (excluding inventory) used in a trade or business or held for the production of income.

- ➤ **Discretionary Earnings:** Adjusted earnings before taxes, interest income or expense, non-operating and non-recurring expenses, depreciation and other non-cash charges and prior to deducting an owners/officers compensation.

- ➤ **Distribution:** Payment to shareholders made from cash available to the corporation, not for compensation and not related to a loan to or from a shareholder.

- ➤ **Dividend:** A distribution of money or property paid by the corporation to its shareholders, out of the corporation's current or accumulated earnings. Only found in a C-Corporation. If there are no current or accumulated earnings, the distribution is referred to as a "return of capital."

- ➤ **Domestic Corporation:** A corporation in the state where it has been incorporated.

- ➤ **Draw:** Found primarily in sole proprietorships or partnerships. Owner receives payments that are not deducted in the income statement but as another form of distribution.

- ➤ **EIN (Employer Identification Number):** *See Federal Tax Identification Number.*

- ➤ **Employee:** An individual that provides services to a business and is distinguished differently from an independent contractor. This is important because the withholding of incomes taxes on wage applies only to this individual.

- **Equity:** The recorded "value" of the ownership interest in a business entity. Also known as Owner's Equity.

- **Estimated (Useful) Life:** Period of time over which an asset will be used by a particular taxpayer.

- **Expense:** An item charged against revenue in the income statement for something that is used up during the income statement period of time.

- **Fair Market Value (FMV):** The amount at which property would change hands between a willing buyer and a willing seller, neither being under compulsion to buy or sell and both having reasonable knowledge of the relevant facts.

- **Federal Tax Identification Number:** This is a number assigned to a corporation or other business entity by the federal government for tax purposes. This is also known as EIN (Employer Identification Number).

- **FICA (Federal Insurance Contributions Act):** The law that provides for Social Security and Medicare benefits. This program is financed by payroll taxes imposed equally on the employer and the employee. A person self-employed will pay both the employer and employee portion of this tax which is known as self-employment tax.

- **Fiscal Year:** Any period of exactly or approximately 12 months used by a business as its accounting period. Some retail businesses always close their year-end on a Saturday and therefore will have either 52 or 53 weeks in a fiscal year.

- **Foreign Corporation:** A corporation not organized under the laws of one of the states or territories of the United States. This description relates to the federal level as this term is also used by each state to describe a corporation doing business in the state but organized under another states laws.

- **GAAP (Generally Accepted Accounting Principles):** A widely accepted set of rules, conventions, standards, and procedures for reporting financial information, as established by the Financial Accounting Standards Board of the American Institute of Certified Public Accountants.

- **General Ledger:** Usually refers to all the accounts established and maintained by the business and includes the balances in these accounts as of a particular date.

- **Goodwill:** The ability of a business to generate income in excess of a normal rate on assets due to superior managerial skills, market position, new product technology, etc.

- **Gross Profit:** That portion of Net Sales that remains after the subtraction of the Cost of Goods Sold. This is sometimes called Gross Margin.

- **Hybrid Method of Accounting:** Combination of accounting methods, usually of the cash and accrual methods.

- **Income:** All sources of business income; may be synonymous with Revenue or Sales.

- **Income Statement (IS):** A financial statement used to report the financial results of a business' operations during the period of time specified within the statement. Also known as the Profit and Loss or P&L.

- ➤ **Independent Contractor:** Taxpayer who contracts to do work according to his own methods and who is not subject to control except as to the results of such work. An employee, by contrast, is subject to the control of the employer as to the methods to be used to obtain the desired results.

- ➤ **Intangible Personal Property:** Assets, other than real property, with no intrinsic value; its value lies in the rights conveyed. Examples include cash, insurance, stock, goodwill, and patents.

- ➤ **Inventory:** List of articles of property. For income tax purposes, this refers only to a list of articles comprising stock in trade–articles held for sale to customers in the regular course of a trade or business.

- ➤ **Joint Tenancy:** Form of joint ownership. Each tenant has an undivided interest in the entire property. On death of one of the owners, the survivor becomes the owner of the whole. This may involve more than two persons.

- ➤ **Joint Venture:** An enterprise participated in by associates acting together, with a community of interests, each associate having the right to participate in its management.

- ➤ **Lessee:** One who rents property from another. In the case of real estate, the lessee is also known as the tenant.

- ➤ **Lessor:** One who rents property to another. In the case of real estate, the lessor is also known as the landlord.

- ➤ **Like-Kind Exchange:** An exchange of property held for productive use in a trade or business or for investment (except inventory and stocks and bonds) for property of the same type.

- ➤ **Limited Liability Company (LLC):** Operating structure contains the liability protection of a corporation and the flexibility of a partnership.

- ➤ **Liquidation:** The process of converting securities or other property into cash.

- ➤ **Listed Property:** Assets that includes passenger autos and other property used for transportation, property generally used for purposes of entertainment, recreation or amusement, computers not used exclusively at a regular business establishment, cellular telephones, and other property to be specified by the IRS.

- ➤ **M & A (Mergers and Acquisitions):** Larger business buy/sell transactions.

- ➤ **Merger:** A merger occurs when two corporations join together into one, with one corporation surviving and the other corporation disappearing.

- ➤ **Modified Accelerated Cost Recovery System (MACRS):** The method of depreciation introduced by the Tax Reform Act of 1986.

- ➤ **Most Probable Selling Price:** The result of bringing together the Fair Market Value of tangible and intangible assets plus goodwill then plus or minus any other adjustments.

- ➤ **NAICS (North American Industry Classification System) Code:** A system of numbering that assigns a unique number to each business industry and thereby allows for collection and comparison of statistical information within an industry. *Also see SIC code.*

- **Net Cash Flow:** Net income plus all non-cash charges (depreciation, amortization and depletion), less amounts needed for capital expenditures, plus/minus net change in working capital, plus/minus changes in debt. (This would be net cash flow for equity, while net cash flow for invested capital would exclude the net change in debt and adjust net income to include interest expense, net of tax.)

- **Net Profit/Net Income:** Total revenues less all expenses. Should always be identified as pre-tax or after-tax.

- **Net Worth:** Total assets minus total liabilities as reflected by the balance sheet. Synonymous with net book value or owner's equity (Balance Sheet term).

- **Net Operating Loss (NOL):** Net loss for the year attributable to business or casualty loss. In order to mitigate the effect of the annual accounting period concept, the law allows taxpayers to use an excess loss of one year as a deduction for certain past or future years.

- **Partnership:** Form of business in which two or more persons join their money and skills in conducting the business. This form is treated as a conduit and is not subject to taxation.

- **Patent:** Legal protection for an inventor. If issued, a patent grants "the right to exclude others from making, using, offering for sale, or selling" the invention. There are three types of patents: design, utility and plant.

- **Prepaid Expense:** The capitalized payment for items such as rent, insurance, etc. that cover more than one year. Cash-basis as well as accrual-basis taxpayers usually are required to capitalize these types of costs.

- **Ownership:** A generic term meaning 100% controlling ownership.

- **Perquisites (Perks):** Special additional benefits received as compensation because of position. In privately held businesses these are often a result of the ability of the business to pay for them, more than a result of market rate compensation for the services provided to the business. For example, company-paid vehicles, insurance, travel, memberships, etc.

- **Piercing the Corporate Veil:** One of the benefits of incorporating a business is that the owners will not be personally liable for the debts of the business. However, if a corporation does not follow such formalities as holding board of director and shareholder meetings and treat transactions with owners at arm's length terms, creditors may be able to "pierce the corporate veil" by taking legal action and seek owner's assets to satisfy corporate debts.

- **Prepaid Expenses:** Expenditures that have a benefit for up to twelve months. Examples include annual property insurance premiums or yellow pages advertising.

- **Recasting:** Changing the amounts recorded in the income statement and balance sheet to amounts that more accurately reflect the earning power of the business and the assets and liabilities that are being transferred.

- **Repair:** A current expenditure to restore business-use property to an original condition or maintain the property through minor alterations rather than to extend its useful life. The cost of a repair is typically deducted annually.

- **Reviewed Financial Statements:** Performing testing and analysis that provide the accountant with a reasonable basis for expressing limited assurance that there are not material modifications that would be made to the financial statements for them to be in conformity with GAAP or some other comprehensive basis of accounting. *Also see Audit and Compilation Financial Statements.*

- **S Corporation:** An elective provision permitting certain small business corporations and their shareholders to elect special income tax treatment. Of major significance is the fact that this election usually avoids the corporate income tax and corporate losses can be claimed by the shareholders.

- **Section 179 Expense Deduction:** An election to treat the cost of certain qualified property as a currently deductible expense rather than as a capital expenditure. This treatment is also referred to as expensing. A maximum deduction, adjusted annually, may be claimed for qualified assets placed in service during the year. This deduction may be further limited based on the total cost of depreciable assets placed in service during the year.

- **Self-Employment Income:** Payment from business activities earned by self-employed individuals and entitles them to social security and Medicare benefits through the payment of self-employment tax.

- **Self-Employment Tax:** Social security and Medicare tax, known as FICA, assessed to self-employed individuals. An employer normally pays 50% of required FICA while the employee pays 50%. Since a self-employed person is both employer and employee, 100% of the tax must be paid by the self-employed person.

- **SIC (Standard Industrial Classification) Code or NAICS (North American Industry Classification System) Code:** System of numbering that assigns a unique number to each business industry. This allows for collection and comparison of statistical information within an industry.

- **Source Documents:** Virtually every business transaction needs documentation which is known as a source document or supporting documentation (back-up). Examples include check register, invoice, receipt, purchase order, etc.

- **Tangible Personal Property:** Assets other than real property that have a physical existence and an intrinsic value. Examples are livestock, machinery, equipment and vehicles.

- **Trademark:** Word, name, symbol, or device that is used in trade with goods to indicate the source of the goods and to distinguish them from the goods of others.

- **Trial Balance:** List of all accounts that have an amount in them on a particular date, showing that each account has either a debit or credit balance. The total debit balances should equal the total credit balances.

- **Working Capital:** Excess of the value of the current assets over the value of the current liabilities.

Other Books In This Series

If you've always thought you would like to own and operate your own business but were never sure where to start, this is the guide for you. This 174 page workbook starts by asking the question if business ownership is for you. It then explains the options available to you and then takes you through, in detail, a step by step process to determining what sort of business you can buy, what you will need to buy a business, and, how to evaluate a business for sale. It also includes the steps to prepare for business ownership with your legal entity, understanding business licenses and permits, how to obtain finance to buy a business, accounting processes and terms, financial planning tools such as profit and loss projectors, sales forecasts, how to create business plans, sales and marketing plans. There are lots of checklists, resources, other planning sheets and tools so when you buy your business you are up and running as quickly as possible for maximum profit.

If you are considering business ownership there are three options available to you. Start your own business from scratch, buy an existing business or buy the rights to a franchise in your local market. This 144 page guide is for those who are considering buying a franchise. The processes can be very confusing and demanding trying to work out the many variables such as which franchise to buy, what franchises are available, what is the initial cost, how much are the royalties and any other ongoing costs and which legal entity to use. It also looks at getting a loan, what the franchisor provides, your role, how much and what sort of support you get. This guide covers all these questions and many more. If you are serious about buying a franchise this guide will walk you through the steps and provide the answers for you from the initial steps to opening the doors of your business while answering all your questions so you do things from a position of strength.

Are you considering business ownership and not sure where to start? If so, you have three options. Buy an existing business, buy the rights to a franchise or start your own business from scratch. This 182 page workbook includes how to decide which industry is right for you, how to create your legal entity, obtain business permits and licenses and business insurance. It also explains how to build your dream business using the solid foundations of a business plan, sales and marketing plan and productivity plan, all dovetailed with financial planning tools such as start up costs planners, profit and loss projectors, sales forecasts, break even analysis and more. It also includes finance options, checklists, resources, other planning sheets and tools to start your business as quickly as possible. Finally, this workbook shows how to do all this and more with the focus that a buyer may wish to buy your business and if so, what processes you would follow to sell for the highest price.

About The Author

Andrew Rogerson currently holds the Certified Business Intermediary (CBI) designation from the International Business Brokers Association (IBBA), the highest designation awarded by the IBBA. Andrew has also earned the Certified Business Broker (CBB) designation from the California Association of Business Brokers as well as a Certified Machinery and Equipment designation (CMEA) from the National Business and Builders Institute. He also has a Brokers license with the California Department of Real Estate.

As the owner and managing director of Rogerson Business Services in Sacramento, CA, Andrew assists his clients with both selling and buying businesses.

Since 1983, Andrew has owned and operated five businesses. At just 27-years-old, he bought his first business, an international travel agency. With hard work resulting in increased sales, Andrew sold the travel agency just two years later for 2 1/2 times his original purchase price.

Andrew's next venture involved owning and managing two retail office equipment/furniture stores, followed by a wholesale travel and tourism company based in Los Angeles that had an annual turnover of $10,000,000. More recently, Andrew and his wife Anne owned an executive suites business in Fair Oaks, CA. Anne operated this business while Andrew worked as an outsourced program manager at the Roseville campus of Hewlett Packard. At HP, Andrew managed a team of 42, deploying a new global call center and support team that included Web developers, technical writers and trainers.

Andrew was educated at La Trobe University in Melbourne, Australia, his native country, and recently completed studies in Business Valuation and Appraisals and Business Brokerage. Andrew and Anne have two daughters, Belinda and Catherine and reside in Sacramento, California. Andrew enjoys flying (he is pursuing his pilot's license) and SCUBA diving as well as sports and politics.

Contact Andrew for Assistance with Buying or Selling a Business

Andrew offers a broad range of services including business valuations, transaction analysis, consulting for business sellers and buyers, consulting for buyers considering franchise ownership and appraisals for machinery and equipment.

The combination of Andrew's hands-on experience in the business buying and selling process, his diverse background in a variety of industries and his international business experience makes him an ideal choice for a business intermediary.

Call Andrew Rogerson at (916) 570-2674 or send him an e-mail at info@Andrew-Rogerson.com to discuss how you can put his knowledge and experience to work for you.

Visit Andrew's website: www.Andrew-Rogerson.com

www.ingramcontent.com/pod-product-compliance
Lightning Source LLC
Chambersburg PA
CBHW081127170526
45165CB00008B/2578